About the Author

JOANNA ROGERS MACY, Ph.D., is a teacher of world religions, active in movements for peace and justice. She is the author of *Despairwork* and *Dharma and Development*, a book about the Sarvodaya village self-help movement in Sri Lanka. Several thousand people have participated in her workshops in the U.S., Europe and Asia. A mother of three grown children, she is currently living in San Fancisco with her husband.

About the Cover

"The Web" by Mara Loft comes from *Facing the Facts*, a series of educational flip-charts about the nuclear arms race and the Nuclear Weapons Freeze Campaign, co-produced by the Traprock Peace Center and the Peace Development Fund.

Despair and Personal Power in the Nuclear Age

Despair and Personal Power in the Nuclear Age

Joanna Rogers Macy

New Society Publishers

Permissions

I dedicate this book to my husband, Francis,
bright spirit, strong arm, lover of life,
and to our children
and their children's children.

Robert McCann

September, 1984

Contents

Acknowledgments

Many hands and hearts went into the making of this book, but there is one person whose help was indispensable. Without Rosa Lane, my editorial advisor, who prodded and guided me through the three months of the final draft, I expect the material would still be in boxes of papers and notes. For your keen eye and ear, for your taste, your judgment, your steady pace and your belief in the book, I thank you, Rosa, poet, builder, strong Maine woman.

Of key importance, too, was my Boston support team of Merloyd Lawrence and Richmond Mayo-Smith. For your guidance, encouragement and material support, I am deeply grateful.

I also thank the *est* Foundation for the grant of funds that enabled me to collect, develop, design and test much of the material that has gone into this book. You saw the value of this consciousness-raising work on the grassroots level, and your support has helped me share it with the broader public.

Despair and empowerment work is a collective enterprise and countless colleagues in the Interhelp network have contributed distinctive and significant insights, methods and experiences. Among these, from the outset, were Joseph and Teresina Havens, Chellis Glendinning, Frances Peavey, John Steiner, David Hoffman and Carol Wolman. Many others since then have enriched the work described in this book: Manya Arond, Ted Behr, Philip Bennett, Joan Bokaer, Tova Green, Paul Fink, Barbara Hazard, Barbara Hegarty, Myra Levy, Kevin McVeigh, Elissa Melamed, Robert Murphy, Margaret Pavel, Sarah Pirtle, Annie Prutzman, Nancy Robinson, Betsy Rose, Molly Scott, Anne Slepian, Mark Sommer, Ba Stopha, Charles Varon, Berne Weiss . . . these names are but a few of the many Interhelp colleagues who have brought to me and others fresh insights and energy in the doing of this work. With you I have been through some of the most potent experiences of my life.

The development of the work has also been enriched for me by spiritual friends both Christian and Buddhist. Some of the approaches and methods were first tested in groups sponsored by the Shalem Institute for Spiritual Formation and with my colleague Father Rich Byrne. I am also indebted to my Buddhist brothers and sisters in Sri Lanka; my year with you in the Sarvodaya Shramadana Movement strengthened me to pursue this work, and in it I adapted some of your methods and meditations. May your merit increase.

Lastly I express my profound gratitude to my family. Thank you Francis, Chris, Jack and Peggy for your loving support and encouragement, and above all for your belief in me and in the value of this work. Thanks, too, Fran, for your editorial help in the last stages of the manuscript. I feel a particular gratitude for my son Jack who, since his first year in college, played a special role in broadening my awareness of the nuclear threat and the environmental crisis, and whose spirit of compassion and clarity ever accompany me in efforts to preserve our beautiful planet.

Introduction

This book is a guide to despair and empowerment work. That term refers to the psychological and spiritual work of dealing with our knowledge and feelings about the present planetary crisis in ways that release energy and vision for creative response. The present crisis includes the growing threat of nuclear war, the progressive destruction of our life support system, the unprecedented spread of human misery and the fact that these developments render questionable, for the first time in history, the survival of our species.

Despair and empowerment work helps us to increase our awareness of these developments without feeling overwhelmed by the dread, grief, anger and sense of powerlessness that they arouse in us. The work overcomes patterns of avoidance and psychic numbing; it builds compassion, community and commitment to act.

The present condition and future prospects of our world engender natural, normal and widespread feelings of distress. Yet, because of fear of pain, social taboos against expressions of despair, and other reasons we will examine, these feelings are largely repressed. This repression tends to paralyze; it builds a sense of isolation and powerlessness. Furthermore, it fosters resistance to painful, but essential information. It is, therefore, not sufficient to discuss the present crisis on the informational level alone, or seek to arouse the public to action by delivering ever more terrifying facts and figures. Information *by itself* can increase resistance, deepening the sense of apathy and powerlessness. We need to help each other process this information on an affective level, if we are to digest it on the cognitive level.

Since 1979 thousands of men and women across the country and abroad have been meeting to deal with the full range of their responses to the planetary crisis. In this work they are drawing resourcefully from general systems theory, humanistic psychology and spiritual teachings. By means of structured exercises, bodywork, guided meditations, rituals and plain talk, they have broken the taboos against expressing their pain for the world, and discovered that they can use this pain in ways which affirm their distinctive gifts and common humanity. They have found that by focusing on their felt responses to the present perils two things happen: (1) Energy is released, for it is with our feelings that our energy lies. And (2) solidarity arises. Discussions and debates on the informational level tend to divide people, especially since argument as to causes, blame and preferred strategies, serves as a prime mechanism for avoidance of painful feelings. When interactions are on the affective level, in a setting of safety and support, mutuality arises between people of differing opinions and backgrounds. In despair and empowerment workshops businessmen and drop-outs, military officers and peace activists, conservatives and anarchists can meet and share their anguish for the future, and find in that sharing common ground and mutual respect.

Meeting in classrooms and livingrooms, town halls and church basements, these men and women, who number now in the thousands, express without timidity or apology their awareness of the threats to human existence and the natural feelings of despair that they arouse. In the process they make some important discoveries — discoveries that often change their lives. These discoveries have to do with their own clarity and courage, with the depth of community they can find with others, and with the power that is in them to act. Together they examine the nature of this power and how it can be lived and applied in whatever projects or programs they choose, for the sake of our planet and its beings.

These projects and programs are manifold, as varied as the lives and work settings of the participants in this work. Calls and letters tell of new neighborhood actions begun, new directions in professional work, new organizations initiated, new study/action groups on campuses and in the workplace. Many simply continue the efforts to which they were already committed, but now with more energy and resilience. Many find that the experience has given them a broader context and fresh meaning to their work as artists and writers, clergy and therapists. And many write that the most telling effect of the work is in their personal lives — in new dimensions of appreciation for themselves and their friends and families.

Writing this book has been a challenge for me, harder than anything I have ever undertaken. The experiences that have gone into it, thousands of encounters and conversations, hundreds of workshops across the country and abroad, were so vivid and vital that to put their essence on paper seemed like trying to catch quicksilver, or pinning a butterfly. I was often discouraged, and even maddened, by the thought that the very process of that naming, describing and analyzing the work would distort it or deaden it. Can we *say* what it is that allows people, by confronting pain, to find power? "It's a mystery — the mystery of life itself," said one workshop participant," One can't explain it, don't try to explain it." Well, I *have* tried — drawing on the spiritual teachings and insights from systems theory that had for me, from the outset, illumined the work. But this attempt is far from the last word. I offer it rather as part of an ongoing conversation, in which I hope more will participate, contributing their distinctive insights and experiences. For this work, however we name it, belongs to us all, by virtue of our being alive together on a threatened planet and of our trying to measure up to that awesome fact.

For some of you this book will serve as a manual for working with other people, either in groups or as individuals. For others of you it may serve simply as a resource in your personal life, enhancing your sense of the global context of your existence. In either case the book as a whole can be useful.

Chapter One starts where we start in workshops: with the recognition of the perils we face, the acknowledgment of the natural responses these perils awaken in us, and a discussion of the cultural and psychological forces that cause us to repress these responses. Just to name them is empowering. In that chapter I also recount the origins of despair and empowerment work, as I experienced them in my life. Chapter Two, on the theory of this work, draws from both science and spirituality to tell us why we can be bold to acknowledge and experience our pain for the world. This pain is a proof of our interconnectedness as open systems, or members of one body, and it can open us to our natural power. The chapter goes on to describe what that power is; so I consider it, in a way, the most important chapter of the book.

The rest of the book consists of applications of those insights. Chapter Three deals with our interactions with individuals in the context of planetary crisis: how we can break the social taboos and talk about it in ways that are mutually strengthening; how we can relate in this context to children and young people, whose chance to grow up is threatened by nuclear weapons; how as helping professionals we can discuss these concerns with people who come to us for counsel. Chapter Four is of particular interest to those of us who facilitate, or wish to facilitate despair and empowerment work in groups; it offers guidelines distilled from my own and many others' experience in this role. If you do not wish to undertake such a role, it is one chapter you can skip without loss, though I urge you to read the section on *Personal Despair and Social Despair*.

The following chapters offer exercises and guided meditations that can be useful to the individual as well as to the group. Chapters Five, Six and Seven describe methods that help us move through the three stages of the work — from the evocation and expression of our pain for the world, to the deepening recognition of its source in our interconnectedness, and then to the articulation, definition and experience of the power of that interconnectedness and its applications in our lives as agents for social change. These tested methods, chosen on the basis of my familiarity with them, are only *some* of the processes that have arisen and proved useful in despair and empowerment work; I am aware that others exist and that new ones will continue to evolve as more and more people engage in the work. The final chapter, Eight, guides us in certain meditation exercises that have proved equally valuable to groups and individuals, as we relate to ourselves and each other in a time of impending apocalypse.

Each new encounter and workshop tells me that this work, as I acknowledged earlier, belongs to us all. It is present in the ways our lives can change, as we open, honestly and together, to the perils and promises of our time. Your thoughts, your responses and experiences, are therefore an intrinsic part of this work. I urge you to share them with the Interhelp network (address in Appendix C), so that they can inform and enhance future editions of this book. Remember that you have something to offer our common enterprise that no one else can offer, and this for two reasons: First, you are an expert by the simple fact that it has been given to you to live on an endangered planet. Each of you awakens each day to a world that could be annihilated at any moment, and you have your own ways of dealing with that — ways that could help the rest of us. Secondly, you bring your own distinctive perspective, as a young person, parent, or senior citizen, as a Black, Caucasian, Native American, Hispanic, Oriental, as a veteran or current member of the armed forces, as a farmer or professional or worker with toxic chemicals or munitions, as a convict or mental patient or public official. What you have to say, as you experience and face what we are doing to our world, has meaning to us all. For we are in this together. If we are to survive, we can only survive together, listening to each other, drawing on each other's strengths.

It is in that spirit that I greet each of you who may read this book. I offer it to you in acknowledgment of all that we have in common, and in love for the world that we share.

Joanna Rogers Macy

San Francisco
March, 1983

Despair and Personal Power in the Nuclear Age

Chapter One

Planetary Perils
And Psychological Responses

I
Concerns For The World

You and I share common knowledge and common fears about what is happening to our world. We live in an extraordinary time — here at this moment on planet Earth. From news reports and from our environment, we are bombarded by signals of distress — of toxic wastes and famines and expiring species, of arms and wars and preparations for war. These boggle the mind and stir within us feelings of dread, anger and sorrow, even though we may never express them. By virtue of our humanity, we share these deep responses.

Let's try something. Take a moment now, take a couple of deep breaths to relax, and let two or three things come to mind that gave you concern for our world this past week. Note the images and feelings that arise.

For some of us, incidents and images may have surfaced immediately. Others of us may still be trying to think of something, while feeling a growing sense of discomfort — even dread. Let me assure you that whatever your response to that exercise, you are not alone. Though our styles of response may differ, we are all citizens of the same planet, all trying in our different ways to cope with a deep, inchoate and collective sense of danger. For to be conscious in our world today involves awareness of unprecedented peril.

This peril, as I see it, comes from three different directions. Each constitutes a development of catastrophic proportion, each increases daily in intensity, and each has become a standard feature in our psychic landscape. Let me review them.

The threat of nuclear war. The U.S. government bases its power and policy on the credibility of this threat. With expenditures in the trillions, weapons of mass destruction proliferate. Nothing in history suggests that they will not be used, or unleashed by accident. Our awareness of this is so potent and pervasive that, according to polls, the majority of the public expects a nuclear war to occur within their lifetimes, that they will not survive it, and that civilization as we know it will end.

The progressive destruction of our life-support system. Toxic wastes . . . acid rain . . . rising rates of radioactivity . . . loss of topsoil and forestland . . . spreading deserts . . . dying seas . . . expiring species of plant and animal life . . . These facts assail us through news reports and our own sensory experience in the air we breathe, the water we drink, and what we see happening to our environment. These developments, arising from our ways of consumption and production, prefigure yet larger-scale disasters.

The growing misery of half the planet's people. Prevailing economic patterns impoverish the Third World, causing hunger, homelessness and disease. In no period of history has so large a proportion of humanity lacked the means for a decent and healthy life. With growing disparity between "haves" and "have nots," with the spread of totalitarian regimes and the use of detention and torture on an unprecedented scale, deep rage erupts, turning our planet into a tinder box.

II
Pain For The World

These developments are facts of life in our present world. They shape the wider context of our lives. Whatever policies we may advocate in response to them, they are part of the story we are living now together. To be aware of them at any level is to feel pain for our world and our collective future. The pain is all the more poignant, since these developments render questionable for the first time in recorded history the survival of our species and of our planet as a viable home for conscious life.

Until now, every generation throughout history lived with the tacit certainty that other generations would follow. Each assumed, without questioning, that its children and children's children and those yet unborn would carry on — to walk the same earth, under the same sky. Hardships, failures and personal death were ever encompassed in that vaster assurance of continuity. That certainty is now lost to us whether we work in the Pentagon or the peace movement. That loss, unmeasured and immeasurable, is the pivotal psychological reality of our time.

"Well, this isn't the first time people expected the end of the world," some of us say. And that is true, at the first millenium and during the Black Plague in Europe there were groups who announced and prepared for that event. But they saw it as the act of a divine being — of a just and wrathful God who was ready to punish the beings he had created and loved. It was seen, in other words, within contexts of meaning that lent dignity and continuity to human lfe. Today, however, the pervasive inklings of apocalypse are bereft of meaning; they are not only bolstered by the projections of scientists but imbued with the absurdity of collective suicide. According to Robert J. Lifton, this sense of radical discontinuity impinges on us all.

> We are thus among the first to live with a recurrent sense of biological severance . . . a radically impaired imagination of human continuity . . . The image of destructive force of unlimited dimensions in both explosive power and in poisoning the environment enters into every relationship involving parents, children, grandparents, and imagined great-grandparents or great-grandchildren.[1]

The responses that arise, as we behold what we are doing to our world, are compounded of many feelings. There is fear — dread of what is overtaking our common life and terror at the thought of the suffering in store for our loved ones and others. There is anger — yes, and bitter rage that we live our lives under the threat of so avoidable and meaningless an end to the human enterprise. There is guilt; for as members of society we feel implicated in this catastrophe and haunted by the thought that we should be able to avert it. And above all, there is sorrow. Confronting so vast and final a loss as this brings sadness beyond the telling.

There are a number of signs that we in America may be on the threshold of a period as a nation when we shall no longer be able to camouflage or repress our despair.
— Rollo May, Freedom and Destiny

Even these terms, however, — anger, fear, sorrow — are inadequate to convey the feelings we experience in this context; for they connote emotions long familiar to our species as it faced the inevitability of personal death. The feelings that assail us now cannot be equated with dread of our own individual demise. Their source lies less in concerns for the personal self than in apprehensions of collective suffering — of what happens to others, to human life and fellow species, to the heritage we share, the unborn generations to come, and our green planet herself, wheeling there in space.

What we are really dealing with here is akin to the original meaning of compassion: "suffering with". It is the distress we feel on behalf of or more precisely in connection with the larger whole of which we are a part. It is our pain for the world.

No one is exempt from that pain, any more than one could exist alone and self-existent in empty space. It is as natural to us as the food and air that we draw from our environment to fashion who we are. It is inseparable from the currents of matter, energy and information that flow through us and sustain us as interconnected open systems. We are not closed off from the world, but integral components of it, like cells in a larger body. When part of that body is traumatized, we sense that trauma too — in the sufferings of fellow-beings, in the pillage of our planet, and even in the violation of future generations. When the condition of the larger system falters, sickens, as is occurring in our present age of exploitation and nuclear technology, the disturbance we feel at a semi-conscious level is acute. Like the impulses of pain in any ailing organism they serve a positive purpose, these impulses of pain are warning signals.

Yet we tend to repress that pain. We block it out because it hurts, because it is frightening, and most of all because we do not understand it and consider it to be a dysfunction, an aberration, a sign of personal weakness.

III

Reactions To Peril

Coming home from school one day, my daughter brought me a riddle: "What is the difference between ignorance and apathy?" I began to answer the question seriously, literally, with definitions and distinctions. But she interrupted me. Shrugging her shoulders, she laughed, "I don't know and I don't care!"

When people talk about public apathy, I remember that riddle and wonder what immobilizes us as a people in the face of imminent disaster. Do we not know? Do we not care?

Yes, we know. Surveys show that two out of three Americans consider that a nuclear war — from which neither they nor our civilization would survive — is likely to occur in the coming years. This is staggering. Yet we look around and see life going on as usual. We continue to pursue the everyday plans and activities that have molded our lives in a routine fashion.

Do we then not care that our world may be destroyed? Of course we care. Look at us — tending our young, planting our gardens, paying our insurance premiums — we have not given up our claim to life. Public apathy in the face of portents of disaster does not derive from indifference.

Apatheia is a Greek word that literally means nonsuffering. Given its etymology, apathy is the inability or the refusal to experience pain. And certainly the pain of awareness in this planet-time is of another dimension than what the ancient Greeks could have known. It pertains not just to loss of wealth, health, reputation or loved ones, but to the extinction of life itself. It is hardly surprising that we often prefer not to feel or even acknowledge it.

Like deer caught or "jacked" in the hunter's headlights we are often immobilized by the fear of moving through that pain. John Mack of the Harvard Medical School tells of the reluctance he felt when asked to head up the American Psychiatric Association's task force on nuclear weapons. He shied from the horror of looking full-face at the Bomb. As he forced himself to do so, he found effectiveness as an agent of change. The study of his task force revealed much about the psychological impact of the nuclear threat, but perhaps the most potent of the findings came from his own experience. "We must seek to embrace the terror and experience its validity," he wrote, "for the immediacy of nuclear death is real. That is the way it is. Only when we can honestly contemplate this horror can we begin to master it . . . until we do so it 'has' us . . ."[2]

As a society we are caught between a sense of impending apocalypse and the fear of acknowledging it. In this "caught" place, our responses are blocked and confused. Look at the following comments that are frequently made when the possibility of mass annihilation is mentioned:

"It's too horrible to think about. I just block it out."
"If I don't think about it, maybe it won't happen."
"Everything I do seems pointless. It could all go at anytime."
"Maybe it won't land here. Maybe we'll survive."
"It won't ever be dropped. No one's that crazy."
"If it happens, it happens. I just hope it's quick."

Do these responses have a familiar ring? Are they a form of *apatheia*? Perhaps you have heard similar comments when issues of human survival surface in the course of a conversation. Try recalling them here.

Looking both at our reactions and our lack of reaction to the peril of our time, we find three widespread behaviors: disbelief, denial and the double life.

Disbelief. Even though much of my life is taken up with this issue, I still find it hard to believe that nuclear weapons exist. Their existence is maddeningly abstract; I've never seen a bomb, let alone an explosion, except on film. I especially find it hard to believe that after millions of years of the evolution of life on earth, after millenia of civilization, of spiritual and artistic geniuses, Shakespeares, Mozarts, Einsteins, we should come to this — that we should be developing and deploying instruments to blow up our world. That these instruments are real, that by human intention they are poised off-shore and targeted at me now, that we are similarly aiming them at conglomerations of other human beings, is — very frankly — a fact that for most of my waking hours I am unable, at some level, to take seriously.

Denial. Such quasi-disbelief can lead, of course, to denial. Until the last few years it was the possibility of annihilation itself that we tended to disclaim. More recently, with the acceleration of the arms race and the talk of "limited nuclear war," we do not deny the danger so much as what is at stake. We hear sober assessments that a hundred million dead are an "acceptable" and "survivable" loss. Stunned by the prospect of so immense an atrocity, the human mind is tempted to acquiesce to the triviality of its own existence. It is tempted to say, as Lifton reports hearing in the halls of his university, "What's so special about human beings?"

Double life. And so we tend to lead our lives as if nothing had changed, while knowing that everything has changed. This is what Lifton calls a "double life", and we all lead it to some extent. On one level we maintain a more or less up-beat capacity to carry on as usual — getting up in the morning and remembering which shoe goes on which foot, getting the kids off to school, meeting our appointments, cheering up our friends . . . and all the while, underneath, there is this inchoate knowledge that our world could go at any moment. Awesome and unprecedented in the history of humanity, it lurks there, with an anguish beyond the naming. Until we find ways of acknowledging and integrating that level of anguished awareness, we repress it; and with that repression we are drained of the energy we need for action and clear thinking.

Each of us has had the experience of responding to emergency. We may have rushed to douse a fire, or pulled a friend from in front of a moving truck, or raced to a child fallen into deep water. Each of us has the capacity to drop everything and act. That power to act is ours in the present situation of peril, all the more so since we are not alone. No outside authority is silencing us; no external force is keeping us from responding with all our might and courage to the present danger to life on Earth. It is something inside us that stifles our responses. What leads us to repress our awareness of danger, miring so many of us in disbelief, denial and a double life?

IV
Causes of Repression

The reasons for repressing our awareness are not hard to find, as was evident in a Despair and Empowerment workshop held in Baltimore. After a morning of sharing deep personal feelings about the planetary crisis, from nightmares of nuclear holocaust to anguish for oppressed peoples, the participants held a brainstorm. The subject: "Why in our daily lives do we avoid expressing these deep concerns?"

Within minutes the sheets of newsprint taped to the wall were filled with dozens of responses, such as:

"I don't want to spoil the time we have left."

"People would see me as a doomsday cartoon figure."

"I don't want to depress my family and friends."

"I don't want to depress myself."

"I want my kids to be happy, I'm afraid of showing them how afraid I am."

"I don't want to get in an argument, and I don't want all the facts and figures about the arms race."

"I'd feel more alone."

"If I spoke my fears, they might come true."

"It takes too much time and energy."

"The future is too overwhelming to talk about."

"I don't want to appear weak or emotional."

You may want to take some time right now to explore your own responses to the question: "Why in my daily life do I avoid expressing these deep concerns?"

You may surprise yourself with how easy it is to answer. There are specific reasons for the kinds of responses we have to this question. And we will be looking at the major factors and forms of fear that inhibit us from acknowledging and expressing the concerns that matter to us most.

Fear of Pain

Our culture conditions us to view pain as dysfunctional. There are pills for headache, backache, neuralgia and premenstrual tension — but no pills, capsules or tablets for this pain for our world. Not even a stiff drink helps much. As Kevin McVeigh says, "Instead of survival being the issue, it is the feelings aroused by possible destruction that loom as most fearful. And as they are judged to be too unpleasant to endure, they are turned off completely. This is the state of psychic numbing."

To permit ourselves to entertain dread for the world is not only painful, but frightening; it appears to threaten our capacity to cope. We are afraid that if we were to let ourselves fully experience our dread, we might fall apart, lose control or be mired in it permanently.

Fear of Appearing Morbid

"Be sociable." "Keep smiling," our society tells us with its cult of optimism. "If you can't say something nice, don't say anything at all," as I was admonished as a child.

I felt that perhaps I was becoming a depressing person to be with, because many of the things I would tell people were not fun to listen to (for example, the connection between nuclear technology and cancer). I even asked some friends if my concern with problems appeared to be getting out of hand, because no one else seemed to care about such things.

—Letter from Louisiana

A sanguine confidence in the future has been a hallmark of the American character and a source of national pride. The successful person, as we conclude from commercials and campaigns, brims with optimism. In such a setting feelings of anguish and despair for our world can appear to be a failure of maintaining stamina and even competence.

Fear of Appearing Stupid

Our culture also conditions us to expect instant solutions. "Don't bring me a problem unless you have the answer," as Lyndon Johnson used to say during the Vietnam war. Similarly today, many feel that we should not complain about a situation unless we have already evolved a "solution" to it. It is hard to express our dread of nuclear holocaust, for example, without finding ourselves enmeshed in an argument over the requirements of national defense and challenged to produce an immediate alternative strategy to secure American power. If we have not evolved a panacea, along with an impressive command of facts and figures about military hardware and the history of the arms race, we can feel stupid, frustrated—as if our concerns were without grounds.

It is discouraging to engage in actions to curb the arms race—or even to express our anxiety about it—when we feel we need to be walking data banks and skillful debaters. Unfortunately, waging peace has become confused with winning an argument.

Fear of Guilt

To acknowledge distress for our world opens us also to a sense of guilt. Few of us are exempt from the suspicion that as a nation, through expedience, lifestyle and dreams of power, we are accomplices to catastrophe.

"I wasn't out of high school when I went to see 'Hiroshima Mon Amour,'" writes Christina Robb in the *Boston Globe*. "I was an American. America had invented, designed, manufactured, used and stockpiled incendiary devices that made the ovens of Auschwitz look like campfires. How could I unknow this knowledge? I didn't want us to be bad. I didn't want to feel so guilty so young. I locked my guilt in with my fear of nuclear war."[3]

Similarly we cannot attend to the spreading hunger in the Third World and our own country — or the trade of toxic chemicals — without feeling somewhat implicated. And that makes their horror yet harder to face. As Peter Marin writes in an essay on moral pain, "Many of us suffer a vague, inchoate sense of betrayal, of having somehow taken a wrong turning, of having somehow said yes or no at the wrong time and to the wrong things, of having somehow taken upon ourselves a general kind of guilt, having two coats while others have none, or just having too much while others have too little—yet proceeding, nonetheless, with our lives as they are."[4]

Fear of Causing Distress

Pain for the world is repressed not only out of embarrassment and guilt, but compassion as well. Reluctant to burden loved ones with our inklings of apocalypse, we would protect them—both from the distress we feel and even the knowledge that we bear it. We don't want them to worry on their own account or on ours. And so, partly out of concern for them, we keep up the pretenses of life-as-usual.

For us parents the psychological burdens of our time are especially heavy and poignant. Not only do the threats to our future hit us with visceral impact, as we picture (or try not to picture) our children in scenes of deprivation and horror; we also try to stifle that dread for the sake of our children's present happiness and sanity. This burden is all the weightier for those of us who believe that it is the role of the parent to be all-wise, all-protective and in control.

Fear of Provoking Disaster

There is also the superstition that negative thoughts are self-fulfilling. "To speak of doom will make it more likely to happen," is the kind of rejoinder many of us often encounter, when we express dread for our collective future.

But in fact it is just the opposite. Psychoanalytic theory and personal life experience show us that it is precisely what we repress that eludes our conscious control and tends to erupt into behavior. "When an inner situation is not made conscious, it happens outside as fate," Carl Jung said. Unfortunately, many of us, ignorant of this fact, make the one who expresses alarm over the prospects of nuclear war feel guilty of somehow contributing to the very fate we fear.

Fear of Appearing Unpatriotic

Deep in many of us, deeper than our criticisms and disappointments about national policies, lies a love of country. It is woven of pride in our history and heroes, of gratitude for what they won for us. Particularly in America, built as it was on utopian expectations, this love of country seems to require of us a profound and almost religious sense of hope—a belief in our manifest destiny as a fulfillment of human dreams.

To entertain feelings of despair over our country's present condition and future prospects seems almost un-American. If I allow these feelings to surface, am I lacking in allegiance? If I express them, am I a peddlar of doom, sapping our confidence as a nation, weakening our will? Am I giving comfort to the enemy? Many would say so, now in this time of crisis. Many would have us silence our fears and doubts, lest they erode our sense of national virtue and our determination to prevail.

In paying heed to these voices, we overlook an essential element in the American character—our capacity to speak out, to "tell it like it is." From the time of the pilgrims we are a people who refused to be silent, who rang alarms with Paul Revere, who called for defiance with Patrick Henry, who with Abraham Lincoln, Emma Goldman, Martin Luther King and countless others gave voice to the future by speaking out. But in this juncture of history, many of us muffle our concerns, shift our gaze, because we are fearful of appearing unpatriotic.

Fear of Sowing Panic

Related to the fear of being unpatriotic is the fear of fostering social disarray. Some of us who are well aware that our collective future hangs by a thread, keep the noble silence of the stoic. Aware that fire is licking at the roof of the theatre, we keep cool and continue with the show, lest panic be sown. What will happen if I speak my fears? Will mayhem be unleashed? We tend to doubt others' capacity to respond to danger in a sane, mature and compassionate manner. Preferring to carry the burden of our awareness alone, we keep a stiff upper lip. Unable to control the forces around us, we try at least to control ourselves, stifling our own alarm.

Fear of Religious Doubt

"God won't let this happen," many of us think (or try to think) when images of mass annihilation break through our defenses. Even to entertain these images, can seem to challenge our belief in a loving and omnipotent deity, and in the goodness of creation itself. Are feelings of despair over the growing possibilities of disaster a sign of inadequate faith?

Throughout history, of course, the fact of human suffering has ever tested our belief in a divine order. The issue is known as theodicy: how to square the existence of evil with an existence of a benign and powerful God. The struggle with this issue has deepened the heart, broadened the mind. It has brought us back again and again to a core truth in each major religious heritage—and that is the deep, indeed sacred power within each of us to open to the needs and the suffering of humanity. That power, a wellspring of love, compassion and service, is proclaimed in the Psalms and prophets of Judaism, in the Cross of Christ, in the path of the Buddhist bodhisattva, in the brotherhood at the heart of Islam... Yet we tend to forget those summons to take within ourselves the travail of our world. Assuming, perhaps, that our God is too fragile or too limited to encompass that pain, unsure whether God will meet us in the midst of such darkness, we hesitate to let ourselves experience it, lest our faith be shattered or revealed as inadequate.

Fear of Appearing Too Emotional

Many of us refrain from expressing our deep concerns for the world in order to avoid creating the impression that we are a prey to our feelings.

For centuries the dominant Western white male culture has erected a dichotomy between reason and emotion. Assuming that reality can be apprehended in an "objective" fashion, it has accorded higher value and trust to the analytical operations of intellect than to the "subjective" realm of feelings, sensations and intuitions. Such dichotomies are no longer found to be valid; for advances in subatomic physics, depth psychology and general systems theory reveal the fallacy of "objectivity." But old mental habits die slowly. Many of us, schooled in the separation of reason from feeling, discount and discredit our deepest responses to the condition of our world. Dread of nuclear holocaust? Grief for expiring species? Horror for the millions in hunger? Those are "just" feelings, frequently dismissed in ourselves and in others as self-indulgent, "idealistic" and "irresponsible."

Given the different ways the sexes are socialized in our culture, men suffer more than women from the fear of appearing "emotional;" displays of feeling can cause them to be considered unstable, especially in work situations. Yet women experience this fear, too. They often withhold their expressions of concern and anguish for the world lest these be treated condescendingly, as "just like a woman."

Lack of emotionalism in discussions about nuclear war is not a sign of reason, but of a sick passivity. — Alice Cook, British journalist

---

Sense of Separate Existence

We have been conditioned to assume—thanks to the individualistic bias of our culture—that we are essentially separate selves, driven by aggressive impulses, competing for a place in the sun. Our affective responses to the plight of our world are interpreted reductionistically in the light of these assumptions, and given short shrift.

We have trouble crediting the notion that concerns for the general welfare might be genuine, and acute enough to cause distress. Assuming that all our drives are ego-centered, we tend to wonder if feelings of despair for our planet are not manifestations of some private neurosis. Do we find ourselves weeping for the Afghans or the peasants in El Salvador, or the decimation of dolphins? Perhaps we suffer from a hangover of Puritan guilt. Maybe we are sexually unfulfilled or toilet-trained too early. Thus we are tempted to discredit those feelings that arise from solidarity with our fellow-beings, dismissing them as some kind of personal morbidity. "Even in my therapy group," writes a teacher, "I stopped mentioning my fears of nuclear war. The others kept saying, 'What are you running from in your life by creating these worries for yourself?'"

Many of us, conditioned to take seriously only those feelings that pertain to our individual needs and wants, find it hard to believe that we can suffer on behalf of society itself—and on behalf of our planet—and that such suffering is real and valid and healthy.

Fear of Feeling Powerless

Probably the most frequent response to the subject of the nuclear threat (or acid rain . . . or world hunger . . . etc.) is to the effect that "I don't think about that, because there is nothing I can do about it."

Logically, this is a non-sequitur: it confuses what can be thought with what can be done. And it is a tragic one, for when forces are seen as so vast that they cannot be consciously contemplated or seriously discussed, we are doubly victimized—impeded in thought as well as action.

Resistance to painful information on the grounds that we cannot "do anything about it" springs less from powerlessness—as a measure of our capacity to effect change—than from the fear of experiencing powerlessness. The model of the self which predominates in Western culture is: "I am the master of my fate and the captain of my soul." It makes us reluctant to engage in issues which remind us that we do not exert ultimate control over our lives. We feel somehow we ought to be in charge of our existence and emotions, to have all the answers. And so we tend to shrink the sphere of our attention to those areas in which we feel we can be in charge.

The great pivotal questions of life require us to stand before them in humility—at least for a moment, naked of know-how and shorn of self-assurance. Yet wanting to believe in our own power and savvy, we shy from what appears, even temporarily, to threaten them.

V
Effects of Repression

Let us now consider the costs we incur when we repress in these ways our responses of pain for the world and alarm for the future. What does it do to us to block out not only deep, recurrent responses of fear, anger, grief, but even the very instinct for self-preservation in the face of possible annihilation?

The repression takes a mammoth toll on our energies. A marked loss of affect results, as if a nerve had been cut. As Barry Childers says, "We immunize ourselves against the demands of the situation by narrowing our awareness." This anesthetization affects other aspects of our life as well—loves and losses are less intense, the sky less vivid—for if we are not going to let ourselves feel pain, we will not feel much else either. "The mind pays for its deadening to the state of our world," observes Dr. Robert Murphy, "by giving up its capacity for joy and flexibility."[5]

This state of absence or at best dulled human response to our world is called *psychic numbing.* Robert Lifton, who coined the term in his study of Hiroshima survivors, now applies it to us all—recognizing that everyone in this planet-time, by simple fact of being threatened with horrors too vast to contemplate, is a victim of the Bomb. "The very existence of nuclear weapons," says Norman McLeod, "is an assault on the human heart." Under such an assault we tend to shut down and finally to shut off.

> *Psychic numbing does not exist at the top levels of government. Of course, if you allow the emotion of nuclear war to enter the Defense Department, you'd end up totally paralyzed.*
> **Wm. G. Hyland, former Deputy Director of the National Security Council**

In the following sections we will be exploring the various forms of psychic numbing in order to put our ear to the ground, and better understand the psychological and even spiritual condition of our time.

Fragmentation and Alienation

We all tend to lead, as we noted, "a double life." While on the surface we focus on business-as-usual, underneath there is an inchoate awareness of impending doom. As with any form of lying, this internal split produces self-doubt and cuts us off from our deep subconscious sources of creativity. Separated from our inner authority, we become more susceptible to panic and mob hysteria.

This split also conduces to a sense of isolation. If our deepest concerns for our world are unmentionable, if we hide them like a secret shame, they alienate us from other people. Although these concerns may seem valid, on the cognitive level, their distance from the tenor of life around us makes us question them on the feeling level. A psychic dissonance is produced that can lead us to question not society's sanity, but our own.

So we seal off, as in an isolation cell, an authentic part of ourselves. "Given the social taboo against crying out (over the threat of nuclear annihilation), people distance themselves from each other as do the families and friends of the terminally ill," says theologian Harvey Cox.

Displacement Activities

Rats in the laboratory, when a threat is introduced that they cannot dispel, are observed to turn away and busy themselves in frenzied, irrelevant activities. So apparently do we. Seeking escape from the "unthinkable," our society turns increasingly to a desperate pursuit of pleasure and other short-term goals. The "new hedonism" evident in the consumption of goods, sex and entertainment—and the cult of the pursuit of money as an end in itself—are so striking today as to suggest that they derive from more than sheer appetite. The frantic quality to it all does not convey a healthy lust for life so much as the contrary; and it suggests a profound doubt in the goodness of life and a sense of impending loss. Helen Caldicott calls this "manic denial."

Political Passivity

To allay our hidden fears about the fate of the earth, there is a tendency to take refuge in the belief that the experts know best. "There are profound, powerful and unconscious needs to see the government as powerful, protective and wise," says Dr. Leon Balter. His report on the New York Psychiatric Association's study of psychological responses to the nuclear threat states that, "People use the presence and fantasies about the government in the service of allaying anxiety . . . Even though its efficacy to prevent war is acknowledged to be faulty, the government becomes the fantasied repository of war-preventing expertise . . . There is (also) an emotional pay-off to have a strong, aggressive government so that the citizen does not feel aggressive."[6]

As we saw earlier, repression of our pain for the world isolates us from others; it diminishes our sense of interconnectedness and solidarity. It, therefore, serves to disempower us politically. To keep a stiff upper lip in the face of adversity is often upheld as a virtue by those in positions of power and serves as an indirect means of control. To do so as millions languish in hunger camps and detention cells, to behold impassively the destruction of our life support system, is to relinquish a measure of our humanity—and become docile, obedient pawns.

Destructive Behaviors

"Repression is never successful," says Robert Murphy recalling Freud's concept of the "return of the repressed." Feelings of despair over the world and the loss of our future may be pushed below conscious awareness, but they surface again in other guises. They are expressed outwardly against society in acts of violence and vandalism—acts often so senseless, so pointless, they seem motivated by nothing so much as fury and futility. And they are expressed inwardly, too, in self-destruction—as the rising rates of drug abuse and suicide among teenagers and even children attest. They cannot all be reduced to idiosyncratic disorders; to an unmeasurable extent they relate to feelings about the kind of world we are living in now.

Psychological Projection

When feelings of despair and pain for our world remain unnamed and unacknowledged, the vague, free-floating sense that there is something intolerable in our situation is turned in anger against others. We seek scapegoats to blame for our inchoate sense of alarm. Carl Jung called this kind of phenomenon "the projection of the shadow."

On the global scene it leads us to "demonize" the Russians, a term coined by historian and diplomat George Kennan, in describing "the distortion and oversimplification . . . and systematic dehumanization" of the Soviet leadership and people, in which many American leaders indulge. Such stereotyping, he says, is both naive and cynical. "Our blind military rivalry . . . our government's preoccupation with nuclear war . . . are a form of illness. It is morbid in the extreme. It can only be understood as some form of subconscious despair."[7]

This "subconscious despair" is at work as well in the attitudes and allegations that increasingly fragment our own domestic scene. The upsurge of racist and sexist resentments, the recent spates of burning crosses and painted swastikas, the hate-filled diatribes against pinkos, queers and other "deviant" minorities evidence an unacknowledged and misdirected dread of the future. Such dread is projected on both sides, fueling not only rage against protesters and activists, but also the angers that some in the peace movement vent on members of the political and military establishments.

Resistance to Painful Information

On the whole, we like to keep calm. It is not our way to scream, or sing Psalms, or call things the most important question in the whole history of the human race—even when the water is lapping round our feet. First one to panic is a wet. **Dr. Nicholas Humphrey**

To the extent that we repress feelings of despair for the world, we tend to screen out the data that provoke them. This occurs on the individual level: people admit with increasing frequency "I don't read the paper any more . . . I tune out the news . . . I can't take it any more, it bums me out." And, what is more alarming, it occurs on the governmental level with censorship and suppression of adverse reports on oil spills, pollution, the incidence of radiation-induced cancer, etc. It is alarming because all living systems require feedback, if they are to learn, adapt and survive. To deliberately or unconsciously block from our awareness the results of our behaviors is suicidal.

Diminished Intellectual Performance

Under conditions of anxiety the data we *do* choose to deal with are not processed well. In a revealing study of a *Bulletin of Atomic Scientists*, social psychologist Peter Suedfeld explored the relation between the imminence of disaster (gauged by how close the hand is to midnight on the *Bulletin's* doomsday clock) and the level of intellectual performance in its editorial pieces (judged by measures of cognitive integration, complexity and tolerance of ambiguity). His conclusions show that at moments of heightened danger the measures of cognitive functioning were consistently lower.

Thomas Scheff in his study of catharsis points out that the repression of strong emotion impairs our capacity to think. It clouds both perception and thought, rigidifies mental responses and results in a loss of intellectual clarity.

Burn-out

When we are concerned enough about the condition and prospects of the world to study the available data, they turn out to be more alarming than most of us had assumed. Many peace and environmental advocates, exposed to terrifying information by the nature of their work, carry a heavy burden of knowledge. It is compounded by feelings of frustration, as they fight an uphill battle to arouse the public. Yet, they view their own despair as a sign of weakness that would be counterproductive to their efforts. In their role as mobilizers for the public will, they don't feel they can "let their hair down" and expose the extent of their distress about the future. The consequent and continual repression of this despair takes a toll on their energies that leaves them especially vulnerable to bitterness and exhaustion.

During the last fourteen years I have worked on and off for civil rights, the anti-war movement, Native American rights, environmental issues, etc. I have often noticed the high casualty rate among movement people—breakdowns, burn-outs, the irreversible damage done to personal relationships, suicides. We must be clear and very honest about where we are right now and we need to acknowledge the darkness around us and inside of us before we can move on. — **Letter from English Professor, Michigan**

Sense of Powerlessness

The conspiracy of silence concerning our deepest feelings about the future of our species, the degree of numbing, isolation, burnout and cognitive confusion that result from it—all converge to produce a sense of futility. Each act of denial, conscious or unconscious, is an abdication of our powers to respond. "I don't think about nuclear war, because there is nothing I can do about it," is the old refrain. In such a way do we choose the role of victim before attempting to organize and change the situation—before even engaging with it.

As Dr. Leon Balter observes, "The perception of objective danger is met by a withdrawal from engagement with it. The most frequent manifestation of this mental process is the assertion of powerlessness in the face of imminent nuclear war."[8]

There is a spill-over effect to this assumption of powerlessness in the face of the nuclear threat. It is discernible in the way we tend to meet other social, political, economic and ecological problems. Though these challenges are more finite and manageable, they are increasingly met with a fatalistic shrug, as if it were naive and fruitless to suppose that we could clean up our air or our water or the corruption in city hall. If, on a deep psychological level, people have difficulty confronting the most fundamental issue of our time—that of the imminent possibility of mass annihilation — they are not likely to feel either inclined or competent to address the myriad immediate issues that affect the moral and physical quality of life.

VI
The Genesis of Despairwork

In the previous pages we have seen and perhaps experienced how we all, to varying degrees, repress and numb our pain for the world. We have seen why we repress it and what that repression costs us as individuals and as a society. We may find ourselves asking at this moment: Is there an alternative? Can we move beyond numbness without succumbing to despair? Can we acknowledge and live with our pain for the world in ways that affirm our existence, that release our vitality and our powers to act?

These same questions hammered in my head as I sat on a Boston subway returning from a day's conference given by the Cousteau Society in the spring of 1977. This conference focused on the theme of planetary survival. Speeches, panels, workshops, and films delineated with horrifying precision the panoply of dangers facing us, from toxic wastes to nuclear proliferation.

I was glad that my teenage son and daughter, who had invited me to the conference, had stayed on for the evening concert; for it was then, as the subway surfaced to cross over the Charles River, that my mind-heart-body registered the effects of that barrage of information. Crumbling under the cumulative effect of the facts I had learned and the pictures I had seen, my defenses gave way, forcing me to face within myself the knowledge of our possible imminent extinction — as a species, as a planet. Tears flowed as I gazed mutely at the faces on the opposite bench and the glint of evening sun on the river beyond. How do I live with the horror of this knowledge? Do I go crazy with it, or do I numb myself again?

In the weeks and months that followed I carried these questions inside me like a bomb in my chest. Bereft of answers, I had no choice but to let them live there pressing against my heart. Even though I attempted to express my despair and feelings of anguish to a couple of colleagues, I was reluctant to share it with those whom I loved most, as if I didn't want to spoil the time they had left. I felt like the sole victim of a unique and nameless disease with no one to share and compare symptoms. Later I learned, of course, that I was far from alone. Others carried, too, like a hidden ulcer, this dread-filled grief for our planet, this sorrow for humanity.

That was made clear over a year later in August, 1978, at Notre Dame University where I chaired a weeklong seminar on planetary survival issues. College professors and administrators had prepared papers to deliver on themes ranging from the water crisis to nuclear technology. As we convened, I took time to acknowledge that the topic we were addressing was different from any other, that it touched each of us in a profoundly personal way; I suggested that we introduce ourselves by sharing an incident or image of *how* it had touched us. The brief introductions that followed were potent, as those present dropped their professional manner and spoke simply, poignantly of what they saw and felt happening to their world, of their children, of their fears and discouragement. That brief sharing transformed the seminar. It changed the way we related to each other and to the material, it unleashed energy and mutual caring. Sessions went overtime, laced with hilarity and punctuated with plans for future projects. Some kind of magic had happened. Late one night as a group of us talked, a name for that magic emerged. Despairwork.

Just as grief-work is a process by which bereaved persons unblock their numbed energies by acknowledging and grieving the loss of a loved one, so do we all need to unblock our feelings about our threatened planet and the possible demise of our species. Until we do, our power of creative response will be crippled.

I felt an incredible relief that maybe I did not have to keep myself "braced" forever against the pain I see others suffering and against potential holocaust . . . .Besides, the tears of relief that keep coming seem to have a life of their own right now — and the relief, itself, is worth it.

— **Letter from California**

As we struck on despairwork, we were not being theoretical, we were groping for an explanation of what had just happened. We knew that it had something to do with a readiness to face the dark and take that darkness into us, that it had to do, in other words, with a willingness to acknowledge and experience pain, and that this pain for our world, like pain for the loss of a loved one, is a measure of caring. We also knew that the joint journey into the dark had changed us, bonding us in a special way, relieving us of pretense and competition. Something akin to love had occurred, an alchemy that caused us to feel less alone and bolder to face without flinching whatever challenges might lie ahead.

This alchemy has happened again and again with groups and individuals across America and in Europe. After the publication of the first paper on despairwork, many hundreds of people — doctors, housewives, convicts, teenagers, factory and officeworkers — wrote to share their feelings of anguish for our common world. In such cases, and they are countless, despairwork has been done alone, in reading and reflection. At the same time workshops sprang up, where people from all walks of life could share feelings of pain for the world and move through this pain to discover together the power that lies within it. Sometimes these workshops have been called "Despair and Empowerment," sometimes "Awakening in the Nuclear Age," and sometimes "Taking Heart." It is after three years of such workshops — years in which they connected in the network called Interhelp — that our experience is shared now in this book.

In helping to design these workshops, with a growing number of Interhelp colleagues, I drew on years of exploring the interface between spiritual growth and social change, years of adapting meditative practices to empower people as agents for peace and justice. Yet the workshops themselves taught me more than I could have imagined beforehand. The thousands of people with whom I have worked in church basements and community centers and classrooms have revealed to me, in ways I had not forseen, the power and size and beauty of the human heart. They have demonstrated that pain for our world touches each of us and that this pain is rooted in caring. They have demonstrated that our apparent public apathy is but a fear of experiencing and expressing this pain, and that once it is acknowledged and shared it opens the way to our power.

There is no birth of consciousness without pain.   — C. G. Jung

---

These many people have demonstrated that our capacity to grieve is fundamental to our capacity to change. As theologian Dorothee Soelle says, "Suffering is a form of change that a person experiences; it is a mode of becoming."[9] I have beheld this "becoming" in businesspeople, scientists, teachers, and parents, seen how our readiness to own our pain for the world, opens us to deep innate reserves of wisdom and courage.

The French editor, Gerard Blanc, in introducing an article on despairwork (called "Travailler avec l'angoisse planetaire" or planetary anguish) called it a rite of passage. He points out that in adolescence we internalize the reality of personal death, and so-called primitive societies formalize this stage through rituals offering access to the rights and responsibilities of adulthood. Blanc wonders if humanity, in our planetary journey, has not reached a comparable stage, since we perceive for the first time in our history, the possibility of our death as a species. Facing our despair and anguish for our world is, in effect, a kind of initiatory rite, necessary to our growing up — to the fulfillment of the promise within us.

As each one of us breaks through old taboos and conditioned responses, we begin to sense this promise within us; we feel new possibilities stir. We are like organisms awakening from sleep, stretching an arm, bending a leg, making sounds.

This book, drawn from the experience of countless people who have engaged in despair and empowerment work, offers tools and insights to assist in this awakening. These can help us lay claim to the psychological, intellectual and spiritual resources that are available to us in this time of planetary peril, and to use them in our own lives and in our work with others.

Chapter Two

The Theoretical Foundations Of Despair And Empowerment Work

In this book, as in the work it describes, we embark on a journey: it is a voyage through our pain for the world and into our powers to heal the world. If that is the case, then the preceding chapter is like the dock from which we launched, and the following chapters our boat's accoutrements and provisions. This one, setting forth theory, is our compass. It gives us our bearings, as we embark in the realm of our deep responses to threats of global destruction. It helps us to see where we are and where we are going. The original meaning of the word *theory* is *to see, to look at*. It is all the more essential since the time in which we sail is a dark one.

With compass, the mariner is able to navigate regardless of the nature of the craft or the conditions of weather. With a theory that lets us see — we can perceive what is at work in us, through us, and for us in this planet-time. It helps us to stay steady and sure. Without it, we risk the extremes of being locked in numbness or swept away by panic as we open to the magnitude of the dangers confronting us.

I
Principles Of The Work

Let's look at what we need to know in order to open powerfully to the call of this planet-time. Despairwork developed not only out of immediate personal experience, but out of lessons and insights drawn from both science and spiritual teachings. As my colleagues and I progressed with the work, these lessons greeted us again and again, like old friends. They are available to each of us — in a sense they are already present within us — waiting to be recognized and put to use.

These lessons are fivefold: Five principles that are fundamental to the work we undertake, to respond to the psychological and spiritual challenge of our time.

1. *Feelings of pain for our world are natural and healthy.* Confronted with widespread suffering and threats of global disaster, responses of anguish — of fear, anger, and grief and even guilt — are normal. They are a measure of our humanity. And these feelings are probably what we most have in common. Just by virtue of sharing this particular planet-time, we know these feelings more than our own grandparents or any earlier generation could have. We are in grief together. And this grief for our world cannot be reduced to private pathology. We experience it in addition to whatever personal griefs, frustrations, and neuroses we bear. Not to experience it would be a sign of intellectual and moral atrophy, but that is academic, for I have met no one who is immune to this pain.

2. **This pain is morbid only if denied.** It is when we disown our pain for the world that it becomes dysfunctional. We saw it in Chapter One what it costs us to repress it. We saw how that cost is measured in numbness and in feelings of isolation and impotence. It is measured as well in the hatreds and suspicions that divide us. For repressed despair seeks scapegoats, turns in anger against other members of society. It also turns inward in depression and self-destruction, by drug abuse and suicide. We tend to fear that if we consciously acknowledge our despair we may get mired in it, incapacitated. But despair like any emotion is dynamic — once experienced it flows through us. It is only our refusal to acknowledge and feel it that keeps it in place.

To speak of sorrow
works upon it
*   moves it from its*
crouched place barring
the way to and from the soul's hall . . .
    — Denise Levertov, from *To Speak*

---

3. *Information alone is not enough.* To deal with the distress we feel for our world, we need more than additional data about its plight. Terrifying information about the effects of nuclear weapons or environmental pollution can drive us deeper into denial and feelings of futility, unless we can deal with the responses it arouses in us. We need to process this information on the psychological and emotional level in order to fully respond on the cognitive level. *We already know* we are in danger; the essential question is: Can we free ourselves to respond? As Andrew Young, former Ambassador to the UN stated at the September 1982 Congressional Black Caucus: "We really don't need an intellectual analysis of where we are . . ." his voice

rising and breaking . . . "We don't allow ourselves to get into situations where we feel helpless and hopeless and somehow it's in those situations that we feel the spirit." And he recalled that such times of darkness, when people wept together in churches and jails, were turning points in the civil rights movement.

4. *Unblocking repressed feelings releases energy, clears the mind.* This is known as catharsis. Repression is physically, mentally and emotionally expensive: it drains the body, dulls the mind and muffles emotional responses. When repressed material is brought to the surface and released, energy is released as well; life comes into clearer focus. Art, ritual and play have ever played a cathartic role in our history — just as, in our time, psychotherapy does too. By this process the cognitive system appropriates elements of its experience, and by integrating them gains a measure of both control and freedom.

I suppose the experience is somewhat analogous to what happens in psychoanalysis: when the self has been confronted, when the hidden has been brought to the surface, the perhaps paradoxical result is not horror and paralysis — they come when the hidden has not yet been faced — but release and new birth.   — A.J. Muste

---

5. *Unblocking our pain for the world reconnects us with the larger web of life.* When the repressed material that we unblock is distress for our world, catharsis occurs — and also something *more* than catharsis. That is because this distress reflects concerns that extend beyond our separate selves, beyond our individual needs and wants. It is a testimony to our interconnectedness. Therefore, as we let ourselves experience and move through this pain, we move through to its source — reach the underlying matrix of our lives. What occurs, then, is *beyond* catharsis.

The distinction here is an important one. To present despair and empowerment work as just one of catharsis would suggest that, after owning and sharing our responses to mass suffering and the prospects of mass annihilation, we could walk away purged of pain for our world. But that is neither possible nor adequate to our needs, since each day's news brings fresh cause for grief. By recognizing our capacity to suffer with our world, we dawn to wider dimensions of being. In those dimensions there is pain still, but a lot more. There is wonder, even joy, as we come home to our mutual belonging — *and* there is a new kind of power.

To understand why this should be so — and what this kind of power is — we must look at the theoretical foundations of the work. For these principles are derived from some of the oldest and most recent insights into the nature of reality. It is important to understand the worldview in which they are rooted. There we find the compass for our voyage, and the understanding we need to employ, in a responsible and effective fashion, the methods that are offered in the body of this book.

The following sections explain this worldview, or theoretical foundation. In the *Web of Life* (Section II) we look at the systematic nature of reality to recognize how our pain for the world derives from our interconnectedness as open systems. In *Passage Through Darkness* (III) we see how our evolution as a species and our growth as individuals takes us of necessity through painful periods of systemic reorganization and confusion, and how in that darkness we can open to greater intelligence. *Power as Process* (IV) describes our power as natural systems — a power or synergy that springs from our interconnectedness and that is far different from our customary notions of power as domination. In *Opening to Power* (V) we become more aware of how this kind of power has been functioning in our lives, and how it is available to be used for the healing of our world. In *Awakening in the Nuclear Age* (VI) we point to the distinctive, historic character of the process we are now undergoing, and the evolutionary promise it holds for us.

At the end of this chapter, we summarize how this theory applies to the dynamics of despair and empowerment work.

II
The Web Of Life

Where do we go from a world of insanity?
Somewhere on the other side of despair.

— T. S. Eliot

What is it that allows us to feel pain for our world? And what do we discover as we move through it? What awaits us there "on the other side of despair?" To all these questions there is one answer: It is interconnectedness with life and all other beings. It is the living web out of which our individual, separate existences have risen, and in which we are interwoven. Our lives extend beyond our skins, in radical interdependence with the rest of the world.

Contemporary science — and this is perhaps its greatest achievement — has broken through to a fresh discovery of this interrelatedness of all life phenomena. Until our century, classical Western science had proceded on the assumption that the world could be understood and controlled by dissecting it. Breaking the world down into ever smaller pieces, classical Western science divided mind from matter, organs from bodies, plants from ecosystems, and analyzed each separate part. This mechanistic approach left some questions unanswered — such as how do these separate parts interact to sustain life and evolve?

A human being is a part of the whole called by us 'Universe,' a part limited in time and space. He experiences himself, his thoughts and feelings as something separated from the rest, a kind of optical delusion of his consciousness. This delusion is a kind of prison for us, restricting us to our personal desires and to affection for a few persons nearest to us. Our task must be to free ourselves from this prison by widening our circle of compassion to embrace all living creatures and the whole of nature in its beauty.   — Albert Einstein

---

As a result of such questions scientists in our century, starting with the biologists, shifted their perspective. They began to look at wholes instead of parts, at processes instead of substances. What they discovered was these wholes — be they cells, bodies, ecosystems, and even the planet itself — are not just a heap of disjunct parts, but dynamic, intricately organized and balanced systems, interrelated and interdependent in every movement, every function, every exchange of energy. They saw that each element is part of a vaster pattern, a pattern that connects and evolves by discernible principles. The discernment of these principles is what is known as general systems theory.

Ludwig von Bertalanffy, the father of general systems theory, called it a "way of seeing." And while it has spawned many derivative theories relating to particular fields and phenomena, the systems perspective has remained just that — a way of seeing, and one which is recognized by many thinkers as the greatest and farthest-reaching cognitive revolution of our time. Anthropologist Gregory Bateson called it "the biggest bite out of the Tree of Knowledge in two thousand years." For, as the systems view has spread into every domain of science from physics to psychology, it has turned the lens through which we see reality. Instead of beholding random separate entities, we become aware of interconnecting flows — flows of energy, matter, information — and see life forms as patterns in these flows. As systems-cybernetician Norbert Weiner said, "We are whirlpools in a river of everflowing water; we are not stuff that abides but patterns that perpetuate themselves."[2]

By these "everflowing" currents, open systems sustain themselves and evolve in complexity and responsiveness to their environment. Interacting, they weave relationships that shape in turn the environment itself. Every system — be it a cell, a tree, a mind — is like a transformer, changing the very stuff that flows through it. What flows through physical bodies is called matter and energy, what flows through minds is called information; but the distinctions between matter, energy and information have become blurred. What has become clear, however, are the principles by which systems evolve — and central to these principles is openness to the environment, openness to feedback. Thus do form and intelligence flower. For it is by interaction that life forms are sustained.

I had the vision that we were going through the same experience that the Native Americans have, from being relatively comfortable and harmonious in our environment we were, very rapidly, in a state where existence was suffering . . . I saw people wandering, lacking food, shelter, and the earth rendered barren, colorless, dry.

As one who grew up in a rural area and who chooses to continue to live close to the earth, some of my strongest feelings of grief are for the possibility of the earth itself no longer existing — so much beauty, so much selflessly given, so many good lessons learned here! I weep.

— **Letter from Montana**

As we saw earlier, the old mechanistic view of reality has erected dichotomies, separating substance from process, self from other, thought from feeling. But given the interweaving interactions of open systems, these dichotomies no longer hold. What had appeared to be separate self-existent entities are now seen to be so interdependent that their boundaries can only be drawn arbitrarily. What had appeared to be "other" can be equally construed as an extension of the same organism, like a fellow-cell in a larger body. What we had been taught to dismiss as "just" feelings are responses to input from our environment that are no less valid than rational constructs. Feelings and concepts condition each other, both are ways of knowing our world.

Thus do we as systems participate and co-create in the living web, giving and receiving the feedback necessary for its sustenance. To convey this dynamic process systems theorists use a variety of images: an open system is like a pattern made by flowing water, or it is like a flame that keeps its shape by transforming the stuff that flows through it. The dominant image is that of a neuron or nerve cell in a neural net. By its openness to thousands of fellow-neurons it gives rise to intelligence. Through symbiotic interaction these neurons differentiate, enhancing each other in their diversity, and weaving an ever richer, more intricate net.

What the systems view makes clear — and this is a key point to note — is that order and differentiation go hand in hand. Subsystems are able to integrate *as* they differentiate (like the nerve cells in the brain). This is in direct contrast to the mechanistic and patriarchal views which assumed that order requires uniformity, the better to be subordinated to a separate and superior will. Here instead, order manifests within the system itself, where components diversify as they interrelate and respond to the environment. Take the physical system of the body. Hands, feet, heart, lungs — each is a distinctive part with different biological functions and purposes, yet they interact with remarkable synchronicity and coherence. We witness an inner ordering in response to the environment and to needs that arise — such as when we run and the lungs quicken oxygen to the blood, or when we automatically extend a hand to someone who has fallen.

In such a way, through such interactions, do we as open systems weave our world, though each individual consciousness illumines but a small section of it, a short arc in the vaster loops of feeling and knowing.

As our awareness grows, so does that of the web, for we are the universe becoming conscious of itself. With sensibilities evolved through millenia of interaction, we can turn now and know that web as our home. It both cradles us and calls us to weave it further.

At a deep, inner level, this is no news to us. We don't need to be scientists or systems theorists to know that our own pulses quicken and our own ideas ignite in interaction with other beings, that in connection we discover our own distinctive gifts. In each of our lives we have tasted that mutuality. Even though we have been conditioned in our culture to have a conception of ourselves as separate and competitive beings, striving at each other's expense for a place in the sun, we know at a deep level of our consciousness that we belong to each other, inextricably. That knowlege is in us because we have experienced it — and our religious traditions attest to it.

I sometimes look at those around me and see the burns, imagine their terror, and try to imagine their pain. I was sitting in a meeting last night — chairing it, no less! — and became overwhelmed by sadness at the thought of those people, those good people, my friends and companions, dying such horrible deaths. — Letter from Minnesota

---

A central theme in every major faith is just that: to break through the illusion of separateness and realize the unalterable fact of our interdependence. This theme has been often hidden and distorted, given the institutionalization of religion and the authoritarian cast it frequently assumed in the last two millenia of patriarchal culture; but still it is there. From Judaism, Christianity, and Islam to Hinduism, Buddhism, Taoism, and Native American and Goddess religions, each offers images of the sacred web into which we are woven. We are called children of one God and "members of one body;" we are seen as drops in the ocean of Brahman; we are pictured as jewels in the Net of Indra. We interexist — like synapses in the mind of an all-encompassing being. Each faith, furthermore, in its core, recognizes that in confusion, fear and greed we forget, and we fall prey to divisiveness. Each faith offers ways to overcome that amnesia, to break out of the prison cell of egocentricity. To awaken us once again to our true community, these traditions offer prayer and meditation, story and ritual, and also — always — moral action.

In our own time, as we seek to overcome our amnesia and retrieve awareness of our interexistence, we return to these old paths — and open also to new spiritual perspectives. We move beyond the dichotomy of sacred and secular. Instead of vesting divinity in a transcendent, otherworldly being, we recognize it as imminent in the process of life itself. Through process theology we recognize that, like us, God is dynamic — a verb, not a noun. And in so doing we open to voices long unheard, and to voices that speak in fresh ways of our mutual belonging. Many women, for example, are bringing new insights born of a heightened sensitivity to the web of life — and these insights are necessary, since the deprivations and hungers of each age shape the messages it most needs to hear. Thus do we begin again to reconnect. That indeed is the meaning of religion: to bond again, to re-member.

III
Passage Through Darkness

How, if we let ourselves feel despair, can we re-member our collective body? How can our pain for the world make us whole again? Or is it part of the remembering?

Processes of growth and transformation are never pain-free. They require a letting-go of outmoded ways of being, of old assumptions and old defenses. As both science and religion confirm, this letting-go can be a passage through darkness.

The living system learns, adapts, and evolves by reorganizing itself. This usually occurs when its previous ways of responding to the environment are no longer functional. To survive it must then relinquish the codes and constructs by which it formerly interpreted experience. Systems philosopher Ervin Laszlo explains this as the exploratory self-organization of open systems; and psychiatrist Kazimierz Dabrowski, thinking along the same lines, calls it "positive disintegration."

My desperation has nothing to do with my past, my childhood or adolescence. Indeed, it has nothing to do with me except that I own it.

All this does not mean that I do not smile or laugh or cry. It does not mean that I do not have friends and a lover with whom I can give and get support. It does not mean that I do not see the hopeful. It simply means that I am dying — dying. And I want so desperately to live.

— Letter from young man in Oregon

This process can be highly uncomfortable. As we open like a wound to the travail of the world, we are susceptible to new sensations and confusions. Bereft of self-confidence and copefulness, we can feel as though our world is "falling apart." It can make some of us frantic; some of us in desperation go mean. That is because the system (i.e. each of us) is registering anomalies, new signals from the environment that don't match previously programmed codes and constructs. To survive then, the system must change. Perhaps like a crustacean or dinosaur, it must let go of its armor, or its mammoth size.

The pressure and promise of life as it seeks new connections, seem then to demand a measure of dying. In our planetary journey we have repeatedly known this dying, in the wheeling and splitting of the stars, in the cracking open of seeds in the soil, in the relinquishment of scales and fins as we crawled up on the beach and learned to stand. Our evolution attests to this, and so does our present individual life story, as we progressively move beyond the comforts of childhood, and other restricting dependencies.

To experience pain as we register what is happening to our world is a measure of our evolution as open systems. This is not only true from the perspective of systems science but of religion as well. How many mystics in their spiritual journey have spoken of the "dark night of the soul?" Brave enough to let go of accustomed assurances, they let their old convictions and conformities dissolve into nothingness, and stood naked to the terror of the unknown. They let processes, which their minds could not encompass, work through them. *Hello darkness, my old friend.* It is in that darkness that birth takes place.

> *"How shall I begin my song*
> *in the blue night that is settling?*
> *In the great night my heart will go out,*
> *toward me the darkness comes rattling.*
> *In the great night my heart will go out."*
> — Papago Medicine Woman Chant

Many religious people are reluctant to acknowledge their feelings of despair lest their faith be shaken, or appear to falter. Yet the very state of facing the unknown, bereft of assurance, has always been recognized by traditional paths as sacred. It is there, says Jacob Needleman, "in that fleeting state between dreams, which is called 'despair' in some Western teachings and 'self-questioning' in Eastern traditions, (that) a person is said to be able to receive the truth, both about nature and his own possible role in the universal order."[3] Jews have known this in the dry, bone-rattling bleakness of exile. And so have Christians in the darkness of Good Friday and the terror-filled mystery of the Cross, where Jesus himself, experiencing the agony of the world in his own flesh, cried out, "My God, my God, why have you forsaken me?" And so it is, too, with the bodhisattva, the hero model of the Buddhist tradition.

The bodhisattva can hear the music of the spheres and understand the language of the birds; but, by the same sensitivity to the web of life, he or she hears also the cries of torment from the deepest levels of hell. All is registered in the "boundless heart" of the bodhisattva. Through our deepest and innermost responses to our world — to hunger and torture and the threat of annihilation — we touch that boundless heart. It is the web we have woven as interconnected systems — or as synapses in the mind of God.

I believe in a God who is grieving deeply for His/Her people, who is calling us, pleading with us to enter into that same grief. My faithfulness to this God has helped keep me true to my grief for the world. — Letter from Minnesota

IV
Power As Process

As our pain for the world is rooted in our interconnectedness with all life, so surely is our power. But the kind of power at work in the web, in and through open systems, is quite different from our customary notions of power.

The old concept of power, in which most of us have been socialized, originated in a particular world view. This view, as we noted, saw reality as composed of discrete and separate entities, be they rocks, plants, atoms, people . . . Whether you were Aristotle classifying these entities into categories or whether you were Galileo or Newton studying their vectors and velocities, this was the context in which you worked. Power, thereby, came to be seen as a property of these separate entities, reflected in the way they could appear to push each other around. It became identified with domination. Look it up in the dictionary; more often than not it is still defined as having your way with other people — in other words, it is seen as power-over. In such a view power is a zero-sum game, "the more you have, the less I have" . . . "if you win, I lose." It fosters the notion, furthermore, that power involves invulnerability. To be strong, to keep from being pushed around, defenses are needed. Armor and rigidity are needed, so as not to let oneself be influenced or changed.

From the systems perspective, this patriarchal notion of power is both inaccurate and dysfunctional. Earlier in this chapter we learned that life processes are intrinsically self-organizing and evolve through the dynamic and symbiotic interaction of open systems. Power, then, which is the ability to effect change, works not from the top down, but from the bottom up. It is not power-over, but power-with; and this is what systems scientists call *synergy*.

> *You didn't come into this world. You came out of it, like a wave from the ocean. You are not a stranger here.*   — Alan Watts

So life systems evolve flexibility and intelligence, not by closing off from the environment and erecting walls of defense, but by opening ever wider to the currents of matter-energy and information. It is in this interaction that life systems grow, integrating and differentiating. Here, power, far from being identified with invulnerability, requires just the opposite — openness, vulnerability, and readiness to change. This indeed is the direction of evolution. As life forms evolve in intelligence, they shed their armor, and reach outward to an ever wider interplay with the environment. They grow sensitive, vulnerable protuberances — ears, noses, and eyeballs, lips, tongues, fingertips — the better to feel and respond, the better to connect in the web and weave it further.

Noting this, we may well wonder why the old kind of power, as we see it enacted around us and indeed on top of us, seems so effective. Many who wield it seem to get what they want — money, fame, control over others' lives. Yes, they do, but at cost — cost to the larger system and to themselves. Power-over is dysfunctional to the system because it inhibits diversity and feedback; it obstructs self-organizing life processes and fosters entropy — or systemic disintegration. Power-over is expensive to those of us who wield it, too. Like a suit of armor it restricts our vision and movement. Reducing our flexibility and responsiveness, it cuts us off from fuller and freer participation in life — and also from the capacity to enhance it.

The power of open systems is not a property one can own, but a process one opens to. It arises in interaction, as systems (be they people, plants, molecules . . .) engage and enhance their own and each other's capacities. Efficacy is transactional. Take the neuron in the neural net. If a nerve cell were to suppose that its power were a personal property to be preserved and protected from other nerve cells, and increased at their expense, it would erect defenses and isolate itself behind them. It would become dysfunctional, as, indeed, a blocked neuron is. Its efficacy lies in opening itself to the charge, letting the currents of knowing and feeling flow through. Only then can the larger system of which it is a part learn to resond and think.

> *Something inside me has reached to the place*
> *where the world is breathing.* — Kabir, Translated by Robert Bly

The body politic is much like a neural net, as systems thinker, Karl Deutsch, points out. Like the brain, society is a cybernetic system, which only functions well where there is free circulation of information, matter and energy. That is how our mind-bodies work. I put my hand on a hot stove and I rapidly withdraw it, because I get the feedback that my fingers are burning. If I were to begin censoring reports from my internal body-system, I might keep my hand on the stove. The free circulation of information is essential to flexibility and survival.

What first frightened me most about the future of our society was when I learned that our government had deliberately suppressed a report about the effects of oilspills on the oceans. There are, of course, many other instances of suppressed information, such as censorship of studies on radioactivity and cancer. I understand that the government does this in order to protect its policies as well as the oil and nuclear companies that help carry them out; but for any system to suppress feedback — to close its perceptions to the results of its behavior — is suicidal.

As open systems dependent upon larger, evolving systems, we must stay open to the wider flows of information, even when certain information seems inimical to our self-interest. What is required of us, for our survival, is an expanded sense of self-interest, where the needs of the whole, and other beings within that whole, are seen as commensurate with our own. Only then can we begin to think and act together. For this we need that "boundless heart" — and I believe we have it within us by virtue of our nature as open systems.

When we open our awareness to the web of life, we connect not only with the sufferings of others, but to the same measure, with their gifts and powers. We experience synergy. Conditioned by the patriarchal, zero-sum notion of power, we are often tempted to view the skills and good fortunes of others in a competitive fashion — to view them with envy and take them as indications of our own inadequacy or deprivation. But as synergistic open systems, as fellow-neurons in the net, we can welcome them as a common resource. We can learn to tap them — like so much money in the bank.

In the Buddhist tradition this is known as *muditha* or "joy in the joy of others." It is the flip side of compassion. If we can grieve with the griefs of others, so, by the same token, by the same openness, can we find strength in their strengths, bolstering our own individual supplies of courage, commitment, and endurance. There are meditative practices for cultivating *muditha,* and I share these in my workshops, as I do later in this book.

V

Opening to Power

How does power as process — synergistic power — power-with rather than power-over — operate in our lives? We don't own it. We don't use it like a gun. We can't measure its quantity or size. We can't increase it at our neighbor's expense.

Power is like a verb: it happens through us.

We experience it when we engage in interactions that produce value. We can experience that with loved ones and fellow citizens, with God, with music, art and literature, with seeds we plant, materials we shape. Such synergistic exchanges generate something that was not there before and that enhances the capacities and well-being of all who are involved. This product could be a meal or a new point of view, a field of potatoes or a group consensus, a symphony or a new appreciation of a symphony. In each case it involves attentive openness to the surrounding physical or mental environment and alertness to our own and others' responses. It is the capacity to act — and to act in ways that increase the sum total of conscious participation in life.

You can know this power most intimately, perhaps, in your relationship to a lover, spouse or child. When you behold them developing their strengths and skills, and see them dare to take joy and risks in life, your sense of well-being is the greater. You know, at that point, the power that consists of enhancing the power of others. It does not originate in you, but you have helped it to happen, you have let it unfold — and it would not have happened without you. You are its midwife, its gardener.

We can recognize this power by the extent to which it promotes conscious participation in life. To deprive someone of their rights and put them in a detention cell is, from this perspective, an exercise of force, not power. It diminishes the vitality, not just of that person, but of the larger system of which we all are a part, and which is deprived now of their participation and resources. The exercise of power as process demands, therefore, that we unmask and reject all exercises of force that obstruct our and others' participation in life.

The concept of synergistic power summons us, it is true, to develop our capacities for nurturance and empathy. This is especially important for those of us who have been socialized to be competitive — and I am thinking especially of men in our society. But it is equally true that this notion of power presents a challenge to those of us who have been conditioned to please, and who have been assigned by society the more passive and nurturing roles. I am referring, of course, to women. For them, power-with can mean being assertive, taking responsibility to give feedback, and participating more fully in the body politic.

'How could you put your life on the line like that?' someone asked Molly Rush, the Pittsburgh grandmother jailed for civil disobedience at a nuclear weapons plant. 'Our lives are already on the line,' she said. 'My choice was only to set some terms on that.'

The recognition of our interconnectedness with others in the web of life does not mean that we should tolerate destructive behavior. On the contrary, we are called to step in when the health or survival of the larger system is at stake. That can involve lobbying for laws, or intervening in a more surgical fashion to remove power from those who misuse it. This is not a struggle to "seize" power so much as to release it for decentralized use in efficient self-governance.

Thus we act, not only for ourselves or our own party, but also on behalf of all the other "neurons in the net." At that point the myriad resources of that net are ours as well — and these include all our differences and diversities.

VI

Awakening in the Nuclear Age

Qum Qum Ya Habibi Kam Tanam
Arise, arise my beloved, how you sleep
The sun and the moon do not sleep
The stars and the trees do not sleep
The lover and the beloved do not sleep
Arise, my beloved, how you sleep.

— Sufi Chant

Through our pain for the world we can open to power, and this power is not just our own, it belongs to others as well. It relates to the very evolution of our species. It is part of a general awakening or shift toward a new level of social consciousness.

I call this movement a "holonic shift," because it can be understood in terms of our nature as "holons." Open systems are holons. That term, coined by Arthur Koestler, means that each is both a whole, containing subsystems, and at the same time part of a larger system. For us those larger systems include our families, our communities, our society and our planet itself. Like cells in a larger body we participate in them and co-create them. These social systems have not yet developed intelligence, as our brains have, because their parts have not yet integrated and differentiated enough for self-reflexivity.

When a system evolves to great complexity, it needs self-reflexivity in order to survive — that is, it needs the capacity to make conscious choices out of all the information it processes. So far this appears to have arisen only in the brains of higher mammals. Hence we have tended to see intelligence as a function of separate brains lodged inside separate skulls. But now our interactions — the ways we impinge on each other through our economic and political and military developments — are becoming so complex and interdependent that they, too, require a built-in, self-monitoring capacity. If we are not to commit suicide as a species, a real measure of self-reflexivity must arise on the next systemic — or holonic — level. Our present modes of social decision-making — even such fine inventions as the ballot box — are too crude, too slow, and too fallible for the alert and responsible self-governance we need if we are going to survive.

Now that next level of self-reflexivity seems, astonishingly enough, to be starting to constellate. A new social self-awareness is emerging, as we turn to each other more and more, sharpening our antennae. Evidence for this comes from many sources. Researchers report a marked increase in the incidence of parapsychological phenomena — that is, a growing number of people acknowledge having experiences that do not fit into our ordinary ways of knowing. Some call this clairvoyance and telepathy, others interpret these occurrences as occult; but these developments are not interventions from a supernatural dimension. They are the gradual emergence of a new holonic level of consciousness, from our interactions as open systems. We are like neurons in a larger brain and that brain is starting to think. I call this a holonic shift in consciousness.

On Despair and Empowerment day the universe chose once more to become self-conscious in several of us who, with mind's eye and breath-body, saw and felt the vastness of our life as all-embracing web. In compassion we acknowledge our interexistence with suffering sister/brother selves . . . — Financial consultant, Washington, D.C.

We also see evidence for this shift in social developments. Look around at the burgeoning of cooperative grassroots enterprises, the rapid spread of consensus decision-making, the growth of worker-shared management, the networking of neighborhood initiatives. This movement is happening from the bottom up, as it always does — and must — in the self-organization of life processes.

We can also see that our planetary crises are impelling us toward this holonic shift. In that sense the Bomb itself is a gift to us. Confronting us with our mortality as a species, it shows us the suicidal tendency inherent in our conception of ourselves as separate and competitive beings, and goads us to wake up to our interexistence. Given the fragility and limited resources of our planet, given our needs for flexibility and sharing, we have to begin to think together in an integrated, synergistic fashion, rather than in the old fragmented and competitive ways — and we are beginning to do that. Once we tune into our interconnectedness, responsiblity toward self and other become indistinguishable, because each thought and act affect the doer as much as the done-to.

Where, then, does despair fit in? And why is our pain for the world so important? Because these responses manifest our interconnectedness. Our feelings of social and planetary distress serve as a doorway to systemic social consciousness. To use another metaphor, they are like a "shadow limb." Just as an amputee continues to feel itches and twinges in the severed limb, so do we feel pain in those extensions of ourselves — of our larger body — of which we have yet to become fully conscious. These sensations do not belong to our past, like the severed leg or amputee, but to our future.

The dark has its own light.   — Theodore Roethke

Within the context of that larger body — or living web — our own individual efforts can seem paltry. They are hard to measure as significant. Yet, because of the systemic, interactive nature of the web, each act reverberates in that web in ways we cannot possibly see. And each can be essential to the survival of that web. In that sense every one of us can be *the hundredth monkey.*

Many of us know the story, it is based empirically on a scientific study. Observing the learning habits of monkeys on a remote Japanese island, anthropologists scattered sweet potatoes for them to eat. One day a monkey dropped a sweet potato in the water and, retrieving it, found it tasted better when washed free of dirt and sand. She proceeded henceforth to wash her sweet potatoes and taught her sisters to do the same. The practice spread throughout the colony. When the hundredth monkey began to wash his sweet potato in the sea, the practice appeared simultaneously on another island colony of monkeys.

Through the systemic currents of knowing that interweave our world, each of us can be the catalyst or "tipping point" by which new forms of behavior can spread. There are as many different ways of being the hundredth monkey as there are different gifts we possess. For some of us it can be through study or conversation, for others theatre or public office, for others, yet, civil disobedience and imprisonment. But the diversities of our gifts interweave richly when we recognize the larger web within which we act. We begin in this web and, at the same time, journey towards it. We are making it conscious.

VII
Guidelines for
Despair and Empowerment Work

We have looked at the theory underlying despair and empowerment work: its five principles and its foundations in both systems science and spirituality. We have likened this theory to a compass. Where then is the needle pointing? How do we steer? How can we use this theory to help us move through our pain for the world?

Five guidelines emerge. They are the basic dynamics of despair and empowerment work, and as such, they are really all we need to remember. These are not steps in a prescribed order, but guidelines to our process wherever we may find ourselves entering it.

1. *Acknowledge our pain for the world.* If it is present, we cannot deny its reality. We cannot make it go away by arguing it out of existence, or burying it inside of ourselves. We can acknowledge our pain for the world to ourselves through journal writing or prayer, and if we choose, by communicating our awareness to those around us.

2. *Validate our pain for the world.* Let us honor it in ourselves and others, by listening carefully and accepting it as healthy and normal in the present situation. To hurry in with words of cheer can trivialize its meaning and foster repression.

3. *Experience the pain.* Let us not fear its impact on ourselves and others. We will not shatter, for we are not objects that can break. Nor will we get stuck in this pain, for it is dynamic, it flows through us. Drop our defenses, let us stay present to its flow, express it — in words, movement and sounds.

4. *Move through the pain to its source.* As we experience this pain, we learn that it is rooted in caring, not just for ourselves and our children, but for all of humanity. We rediscover our interconnectedness with all beings. Allow this sense of mutual belonging to surface in whatever words and images are meaningful and share them.

5. *Experience the power of interconnectedness.* Let us dare to translate our caring into a sense of belonging to all humanity and the web of life. Observe the trust level rise when we expose our vulnerability to pain for the world. Recognize how the realization of interconnectedness results in personal security and economy of fort.

Particular ways in which we can let this happen are detailed in the following chapters. Whatever words, methods, or exercises we use, however, let us be aware that what is at work in this process is not dependent on what we know or say or do, as much as on what we allow to happen. Neither is despair and empowerment work dependent on group participation. It is a process which can happen in our solitude and in accordance with our own timing. Moving through our pain for our world is no more our doing as separate egos, than childbirth is the doing of the mother. For it is the deep ecology of life itself, if we let it, that draws us home to the awareness of our true nature and power.

Chapter Three

Despair and Empowerment Work
With Individuals

Threats of annihilation form the backdrop of our lives; they are there on the horizon of every relationship; every encounter is, in a sense, silhouetted against them. Yet we find these perils hard to mention. As we saw in Chapter One, our difficulties in acknowleding them to ourselves and to each other serve to isolate, anesthetize and disempower us.

In workshops where we do despair and empowerment work in groups, we find the invigorating sense of reality and community that comes from sharing honestly our inner responses to these dangers. As we prepare to return to our daily lives, one kind of question surfaces more frequently than any other. How do we talk to other people? How can we communicate our shared concerns for the future without triggering rejection or arguments? In talking with friends, family, colleagues, how can we overcome their resistance, and our own, too? How can we face these dangers consciously and openly with other people?

In this chapter we address these questions. First, in Section I *Speaking About the Unspeakable*, we look at how we can bring our planetary concerns into our ordinary communications with the people in our lives — breaking the ice, dealing with argument, and empowering people through listening. Then in Sections II and III, we examine these questions as they arise in two particular areas: in our relations as teachers and parents with children and young people; and in our relations as counselors with clients and others who come to us for guidance.

I
Speaking About the Unspeakable

The issue of human survival can be hardest to talk about with the people in our daily lives. In ordinary conversation it is as taboo as the subject of sex was in the Victorian era. In section III of Chapter One, we saw why this is so, and what fears hinder us from acknowledging and expressing our deep concerns for our common future. Often, when we *do* take courage to talk about them, we find people shrugging their shoulders and changing the subject. Sometimes we find ourselves in an argument and we feel at a loss as to how to convey our views and sense of urgency. In those cases it is easy to forget that peacemaking is different from winning an argument.

We are not talking about a new, more effective propaganda campaign to win hearts and minds . . . the hearts and minds of the people we are talking to belong to the people we need to reach. We need to touch people and leave the changing up to them.
— Wendy Mogey, New Manhattan Project

Let us look at how we can help each other share our responses to the threats of annihilation in ways that are strengthening and bonding.

1. Breaking the Ice

"How's everything?" "Just fine, thanks. And you?" "That's great." This level of dialogue is a common courtesy, and we don't want to lose it. To remain there, however, leaves each party unengaged on the level of their concerns for the world and alone with their fears. But we don't know how to move into *that* subject. How do we mention the unmentionable, especially when others seem oblivious of it?

We cannot simply knock on our neighbor's door and say "The world is standing on the brink of the final abyss" — I thought you'd like to know.
— Dr. Nicholas Humphrey, British scientist

"Many of us who try to talk to our family and friends about our concerns for the world, try to give information or argue policy. It doesn't work," says my colleague Barbara Hazard. "And the more emphatically we try to give the information, the less it seems to work. Something else is operating." That something else, as we saw in Chapter One, is the resistance bred by dread. What we have to do, Hazard says, is to relate to what people already know and feel, and to "look for the core of truth."

Everyone cares. That is one truth we have learned in despair and empowerment work. No one wants our world to die, and everyone, at some level, is afraid that it may. Do not make the error of assuming that people are indifferent. Their age, class, color, sex, uniform, occupation, lifestyle or previous behavior can lead us into unwitting suppositions that are very far from their true fears and feelings.

A second truth is that everyone, at some level, feels lonely and isolated facing the dangers that beset their world. And a third is that everyone wants to break out of that isolation cell.

What we need to do, therefore, is to elicit their concerns about the world and its future, rather than impose our own information. Each of us needs to use ways that are natural for us. For example, concerns can be drawn out with simple questions that reveal our own state of mind.

"Does hearing the news scare you as much as it scares me?"

"Do you also worry about nuclear war sometimes?" (. . . or the toxic wastes?)"
"What is the hardest part for you?"

It can be equally effective, and for some people more honest, to open with simple statements about what is on your heart and mind. If you heard that your mother had cancer, you would, in most cases, not be afraid to express your dismay; your distress for the world is as legitimate a feeling.

"I find myself worrying more and more about our world situation, and it feels like I can't do anything about it."

"I feel sick about the arms race (or the new nuclear plant) and I'd like to talk about it."

More often than not people are relieved when you bring up these concerns in a genuine, personal fashion — and when they know you are not trying to "sell" your political views. Whether or not they say so, they will know then that they are not alone in their fears and they will appreciate the fact that you respect and trust them enough to share your own. Otherwise how will they know you care?

Furthermore, by approaching them on the level of shared concern, we can avoid argument. One can argue policies, strategies, analyses, but not feelings. They are a personal reality, beyond debate. They can be expressed without apology or controversy, because they just "are." Workshop participants have written to me that "People express relief at the mere mention of despairwork." Simply to say that you are addressing, exploring or reading about the psychological effects of the world situation can provide an invitation to others to disclose their own feelings.

This was dramatized to me in an encounter at my daughter's college. Visiting there, I sat in on her course in Introductory Psychology. It occurred to me that the professor, who was entertaining and articulate, could help me clarify my understanding of the dynamics of repression and projection. "I'm working with people on the psychic effects of the nuclear threat and other dangers," I explained, as I asked if I could consult him later in the day, "and I'm not sure I'm using the term 'repression' correctly."

The conversation in his office lasted almost three hours. After I briefly stated the points on which I wanted guidance, he closed the door, took the phone off the hook, and began to talk, ignoring the specific questions I had raised. It was well-meaning, but also naive of me to suppose, he said, that by my work I could turn the tide; for it was too late. There is no hope that we can survive. He had been a social activist himself in the late sixties, but now he knew the absurdity of trying to affect the entrenched power of the military-industrial complex, and he had an awesome command of facts and figures to sustain that view. It is only a matter of time before we all blow up. "And don't worry about your daughter suffering in the nuclear blast," he said. "Here in Connecticut, with our targeted munitions plans, she will be incinerated instantly."

I asked him when he first became aware of this threat, and he described the civil defense drills he had experienced as a child in the fifties. "I was eleven years old. I would lie awake at night. I felt my world had become unglued." And he described how he himself felt "unglued" at that time — "as if the molecules of my body, the cells of my brain no longer cohered, but were scattered already in anticipation of the blast."

Though he now, as a respected member of his department, taught courses that were popular and heavily enrolled, he lived with dread. "Funny, you should come this week," he said, "because, just Tuesday again, when I crossed the campus on my way to class, I saw the buildings crumble. The library and the science building, they just began to go in a cloud of dust. I stopped dead and closed my eyes — and for a moment I was afraid to open them again." As we parted and exchanged addresses, he again warned me against thinking that my work could make any difference. "It's too late." Seared by the passion of his bitterness and grief, I could not argue.

Two months later I received a letter from him. It enclosed an article that dealt eloquently with the civil defense plans for the city and summoned local citizens to back the Nuclear Freeze. In his letter he mentioned a new syllabus he had drawn up for a course, which would help students deal with the nuclear threat. "Our conversation," he wrote, "was a turning point in my life." As I read his words, I recalled that I had said very little. I had not argued with his deep despair; I had simply been there, creating an occasion for him to hear what was in his heart. When I visited my daughter again a year later, he left word with her that he wanted to see me. He showed me the manuscript of a book he had begun on the psychological obstacles to disarmament.

2. Dealing with Differences of Opinion

Many of us are reluctant to reveal our concerns over world issues because we don't want to get into an argument, especially with people who are important to our lives, be they coworkers or employers, relatives or neighbors. We can be afraid of triggering their angers or suspicions. We can be afraid of not knowing enough facts to sustain our views, thereby losing their respect, or we can be afraid of appearing judgmental or self-righteous.

I felt all of these trepidations when, in the last year of the Vietnam war, my husband and I decided to go from house to house in our neighborhood to collect money for candidates who opposed the war. With neighbors who had given us a hand in the snow, whose children played with ours, I feared straining our relationships by politicizing them. I was concerned that we might jeopardize the easy give-and-take by pushing them to declare themselves on a sensitive issue of national policy. As my husband and I knocked on familiar doors and explained our purpose, we found that some gladly gave while others chose not to; but those who declined our request did not argue or seem irritated. People in both categories showed interest, and even appeared to welcome the shift in our relationship into a new area where they learned about our concerns and could share theirs.

Often where there are differences of opinion, say on the issue of disarmament, people are not averse to hearing our views and are more interested in talking than we might expect. We only need to overcome our fears of exposing ourselves. Sometimes, however, we do land in controversy. We get embroiled in debates that become heated and fruitless, and that leave each party more entrenched in their opinions. At this time of critical choices, how can we discuss our differences without polarizing them?

This question has preoccupied a number of peace advocates, including Wendy Mogey and Patsey Leakey of the New Manhattan Project and Lee Stern of the Fellowship of Reconciliation. From them and from my colleages in Interhelp come the following nine suggestions:

1. *Beware of labels and hidden assumptions,* that the person with whom you are talking is a "hawk" or a "dove", that they automatically agree or disagree with your views.

2. *Don't play "total expert."* People see you as more trustworthy if you acknowledge that you don't know. Wendy Mogey says, "By admitting that you don't know the whole story and still can believe that we need to reverse the arms race, you are affirming for people that one doesn't have to be an expert on the technological level in order to support disarmament."

3. *Do your homework,* however, so that you can be responsible for what you say. You do not need many facts and figures to know that our future is becoming ever more insecure.

4. *Be clear whether you are communicating facts or feelings:* the first are debatable and the other not. The statement that "nuclear war is inevitable" can be challenged, but not the assertion, "I am afraid that a nuclear war will happen." Feelings are "givens"; we can report them with varying degrees of ac-

curacy and honesty, but they are not debatable.

5. *Don't try to corner the other person,* backing him or her into a position from which it is hard to change.

6. *Don't be afraid to share personal experiences.* The dangers we are dealing with are abstract and remote from daily life; facts and figures about them take on reality for people when they see that we care, and why we care, and what has led us to the views we hold.

7. *Don't be afraid to examine differences.* If you begin by ascertaining areas of agreement (e.g. "Nuclear war is possible" or "America should be protected"), both parties can trust each other more and proceed to see where their views diverge. The definition of argument is to "give reasons", and this can be an act of respect for both yourself and others. Argument in this sense is healthy and useful: it reveals information gaps (a person, for example, may simply not have known the extent of nuclear proliferation or the health effects of uranium mining), and it leads to reappraisal of old assumptions (that more bombs bring more security, for example, or that the Russians cannot be trusted to keep an arms agreement).

8. *Be willing to let go of a discussion at the right time.* There is a moment when it is best to leave things as they are, in order to allow inner change to occur. And you may never know if change *has* occurred as a result of your discussion. To develop patience, it might help to trace those experiences when you went through personal change and the "change agent" — a book, a film, a speaker, an encounter — had no idea you were affected.

9. *Shift, if you can, to the level of deep common concern.* It is on that level of shared humanity that we can move beyond our differences of opinion and background about the planetary crisis, and sense our solidarity and mutual need. This shift of gears can occur at any point in a discussion — even after you have "lost" the argument.

On a plane trip across the country I found myself in a debate with the man beside me. Seeing the literature on my lap and overhearing me talk about the peace movement with the man on my other side, he finally interrupted to express his amused scorn at "you idealists" who don't realize the imperative for strong defenses against Soviet aggression. He was a security expert working on a military contract, he explained, and so he knew the "facts." Well, I had some facts, too, and I began to point out the economic costs of the arms race, the dangers of accidental launchings, and the inconsistencies in his notions of security. I got nowhere. He kept reiterating his views on the necessity of building up our arsenal. Weary and frustrated, I subsided into silence. As we began the long descent into Newark, I glanced at his averted face — father, he had said, of two young sons. I felt a sudden compassion. "It's a grim outlook," I said, "that your kids and mine will have to live their lives under the constant threat of extinction." "It is worse than you think," he replied, "a lot worse — it will come before *my* kids can even grow up." "That's hard knowledge to live with," I said. Nodding in agreement, he began slowly to share what it felt like — and he did it with a quiet and infinite sadness. "Usually I just shut it out," he said; but for those moments he hadn't, and we had connected on a far deeper level than our conflicting views of national security.

It was not when I argued that he saw the bleak and fragile kind of security that is bought by nuclear threats; and it was not through my voice but his own that he heard it. He could listen to it, because we had shifted below the level of debate, and because I listened, too.

3. Learning to Listen

If it is true, as I have become convinced, that everyone at some level feels distress over the world's future, then we all have a lot to say to each other — once we break through the fears and taboos that keep us silent. Indeed, it is often in the act of expressing our deepest concerns that we discover what we feel and know. Furthermore, in the process of communicating them, change occurs: new ideas and new visions arise. And they are much more compelling than what others may be trying to tell us. Perhaps the greatest value of despair and empowerment work is the opportunity it provides for people to hear *themselves* — and "come home" to the perceptions and truths they have garnered by living every day and night on a threatened planet. For this to happen, the art of listening is essential. It reveals and it empowers. I have come to believe that it is the most powerful tool in peacemaking and any other kind of social change work.

It is not a passive undertaking; it takes alertness and energy, as the phrase "active listening" suggests. It requires concentration, and a measure of confidence and even courage, to hear a person without interrupting or mentally preparing our own reply. "Few of us are really good listeners . . . . It is not a skill that comes naturally," says psychologist Barry Childers, who offers the Listening Workshop to educators, health practitioners and community organizers, "Good listening is the most important ingredient in any helping relationship."

"When a person feels safe to express his or her own views and feelings, without being judged or redirected, that person is more apt to say what is *really* going on," says psychotherapist Dr. Michael Diamond. And in this time of planetary crisis, we need more than ever to know "what is really going on."

The impact of someone's failure to listen . . . the absence of response has painful numbing consequences.
— Clark Moustakis, from *"Who Will Listen"*

Let me tell you about three champion listeners I know in the Interhelp network.

One is Mark Sommer, a writer and peace advocate who took off one fall to ride the trains with a tape recorder. Striking up conversations in the club car, he explained that he wanted to find out what people thought about the arms race and the prospects for the world's future. He found people eager to talk; the taped interviews were very moving and often lasted an hour or so. Whether Sommer publishes these interviews or not, they have already effected change — by letting the interviewees themselves hear what they knew and felt.

The bravest listener I know is Frances Peavey, who undertook a world tour to find out what ordinary people thought about the prospects for our planet. In Tokyo, Bangkok, Delhi, she sat on a bench in a central square with a sign beside her. The sign read: "American Willing to Listen." People lined up in queues so long that often she was there on her bench till one or two in the morning. She did not pretend to be an important official or a famous author; "I'm just an ordinary citizen," she would say, "But I want to know what people are thinking;" and she would take notes. In Delhi she met the representative from Tonga, who was attending the world conference of Nonaligned Nations. The delegate was so struck by the role that Peavey had taken on that she set up a table for her in the lobby of the hotel where the conference was being held. Peavey came every afternoon at four, when the Tonga representative brought up one delegate after another for the simple but rare opportunity to talk to an "American willing to listen."

My third champion listener is Norie Huddle of the New Committee on National Security. With her tape recorder she travelled the U.S. to interview people from all walks of life. "What do you think would make America strong?" she would ask. Sometimes the immediate answers were knee-jerk reactions about building up our defenses and being ready to "nuke" the Russians. But Huddle would just listen with avid interest: "And then?" As people experienced themselves being *heard*, without rebuttal or interruption, they would go on talking and often find their ideas moving in new directions. "This is crazy," a truckdriver would say, who had been ready to nuke the Russians, "What a world to leave our kids. You know, maybe we could have an exchange with the Soviets — their young people coming over here, ours going over there — to know each other better and reach some kind of agreement so we could survive." If Huddle had approached him to sell such an idea ("Let me interest you in an exchange program with the Soviet Union"), that same person might well have rejected her, branding her as a "pinko". By virtue of her listening, he heard it from himself, gained respect for his own ingenuity.

The art of inquiry — and listening — raises consciousness. It played an important role in the development of the women's movement. Taking cues from that, psychiatrist Carol Wolman and her colleague Natalie Shiras initiated nuclear consciousness-raising groups in 1977 and 1978, that were some of the early steps in the development of despair and empowerment work. Leading a number of groups in schools and industries, they developed a series of questions to help people break out of passivity, silence and isolation, to experience community, and to empower each other to act. These questions are offered here, because they can be useful to each of us in connecting with our fellow-citizens, whether in groups or as individuals.

Note: *NW* refers to nuclear weapons

1. How long do you expect human life as we now know it to survive?

2. Do you think the danger of nuclear war is going down, up, or is unchanged?

3. What do you expect the world to be like after nuclear war?

4. What are your earliest memories of NWs? What is the history of your awareness of NWs?

5. Have you ever had fantasies, dreams, or nightmares about NWs?

6. How have your personal life choices been affected by the existence of NWs, including choices about children, work, and where you put your energy?

7. How well informed are you abut NWs compared with other areas of public affairs? If there is a discrepancy, how do you explain it?

8. What do you remember about the Cuban missile crisis?

9. If you are active in working against NWs, how do you feel about people who are not? If not, how do you feel about people who are?

10. Do you believe that you need to understand science or political science to take a position on NWs?

11. Do you trust the political, military, scientific, and business leaders who are in control of decisions about NWs?

12. Do you believe that you can influence these decisions?

13. Does your age, sex, ethnic background, social class influence the way you think about NWs?

14. What special relation, if any, do we as Americans have to NWs?

15. Does our culture help you either to be aware of or to forget about NWs?

16. Are you aware of any ways in which you personally participate in the existence of NWs — e.g., via taxes or your job?

17. Do you think that the world is qualitatively different since NWs were invented? If so, how?

18. How does living in the nuclear age change human experience? (People over 40 may have special contributions in answering this question.)

19. Have you ever, before today, discussed your personal thoughts and feelings about NWs with others? If not, why not?

20. Have you talked to your mate, parents, children, friends, coworkers about NWs?

21. Are you worried that you'll be labeled in some way (e.g. communist, crazy, spoilsport, coward) if you talk about NWs?

22. What would you need in the way of support from others to help you speak up more?

23. What gives you hope, strength, courage?

24. What have you done that has been successful in changing something for the better?

25. What do you do to affirm life? Does it either increase or decrease the chances of nuclear destruction?

26. How do you feel about this consciousness-raising format? Do you have ideas for improving it?

27. Would you like to participate in another, or longer term, consciousness raising group?

II
Relating With Children
And Young People

The horror their children may have to face is the most piercing grief for many parents, and would-be parents, as I have seen them contemplate the future. The most intense anger I have witnessed is that of young people as they imagine being robbed of their chance to grow up. Fear of these shattering emotions keeps many of us — adults and youth alike — in silence. That fear is a major source of repression, evasion and numbness in facing the nuclear threat and other critical challenges.

There are times I look at my two children, young, vital and innocent and feel as if my heart is going to explode out of my chest . . . . I do not mind so much for myself having to confront this thing, but I just can't deal with the fact that they might have to and in a far worse form than I . . . I find my chest just heaving, with a tremendous weight, my shoulders are pulled up and taut and there is this core of a knotted pain smack in the middle of me.
— **Letter from a father in British Columbia**

For adults, especially parents and teachers, the danger to our planet is an agonizing issue. We want to protect and reassure our children, but we face dangers from which we cannot protect them and about which we cannot honestly reassure them.

"What can I say to my kids? I want them to be happy, to feel safe."

"I feel guilty somehow—guilty about the kind of world we're handing them, and deceptive that this is one area I am not being honest with them about what I know and feel."

"I don't want to spoil their childhood by bringing up fears they can do nothing about. But, I wonder, am I protecting them or myself?"

So, desirous of protecting our children (and ourselves) we tend, by and large, to remain silent. But are they ignorant of the mounting dangers we face? Do they really not know?

Much has been learned recently of what children and young people *do* know and feel about the precarious condition of our world. Evidence pours in that, although they may not reveal it to the adults in their daily lives, they are very aware of the dangers of imminent mass annihilation. From four, five and six years old, says Robert Lifton, a child knows about nuclear bombs and what they can do. "It is everywhere in our culture," he points out, in television, posters, magazines, even comics. Global Education Associates invited 5th grade children to share their visions of the future, making no reference to negative factors or disaster of any kind. Yet ninety percent said they expected a nuclear war, in which they would not survive. The only hope that some saw lay in an extraterrestrial rescue mission. A task force of the American Psychiatric Association surveyed grammar and high school students with a thousand questionnaires sent to many localities and a hundred interviews in the Boston area. The results showed that the children were well aware of the nuclear threat, and that, furthermore, it had deeply penetrated their consciousness. Some said they did not intend to have children, since it would be unfair to bring them into such a dangerous world. As similar studies and interviews show, children and young people have not much trust that the world will be inhabitable by the year 2000. They have apocalyptic nightmares and daytime flashes of a nuclear holocaust. "And I won't take cover when it comes . . . all that suffering . . . I just hope I vaporize quick."

One night, my son, as if reading my thoughts, blurted out sentences like "When will I die? Who will play with my toys when I die? and I don't want to die for a long time." Ordinarily, such queries would seem healthy and I could respond with an adequate answer. But that night, I couldn't talk. Rather, convulsive sobs came out, half-choked,

*then growing fuller until I held my little boy in fear and desperation
and it was he who reassured me it was all okay and to stop crying.*
— **Letter from New York**

While we prefer to imagine that we can shield our children from the knowledge of what may befall us, we cannot; for they, too, feel despair for the future. In fact, they feel it more keenly than most adults, because they have developed fewer defenses; they are not as numbed as we. Grownups depersonalize the peril, talk in abstract terms about "megatonnage" and "delivery systems" and "nuclear exchanges" and "limited war," while the children see it in concrete terms of burning flesh, searching parents, disintegrating bodies, boiling blood, screams for help. For proof of this, see "Growing Up Under the Shadow," a documentary of interviews with children.

Eric Chivian, staff psychiatrist of the Massachusetts Institute of Technology, who has interviewed many school children in his work with Educators for Social Responsibility, describes how they deal with the knowledge at different stages of their development. He says that at the third grade level there is a marked sense of confusion, hopelessness and fear of abandonment. Nightmares occur, and the realization that they may not live to grow up. By the fifth grade children have more information, and feel anger at the stupidity and hypocrisy of the adult world. By the seventh grade this anger turns to cynicism and gallows humor. Civil defense programs strike them as ludicrous and they attempt to devise solutions; maybe we could erect a giant protective bubble over the country or go live in the sea. In high school the emotional reactions become more complicated. These teenagers face critical choices about college, careers, families, draft registration, but the shadow of the bomb robs these choices of reality and meaning; the young people begin to erect defenses of indifference and defiance.

"It seems that these young people are growing up without the ability to form stable ideals, or the sense of continuity upon which the development of stable personality structure and the formation of serviceable ideals depend," states Dr. John Mack, one of the authors of the American Psychiatric Association's Task Force Report *The Impact on Children and Adolescents of Nuclear Developments.* "We may find we are raising generations of young people without a basis for making long-term commitments, who are given over, of necessity, to doctrines of impulsiveness and immediacy . . . At the very least, we need to educate our children in the realities of nuclear . . . weaponry so that they can be hoped to overcome at least that aspect of fear which derives from ignorances and which leaves them feeling so powerless."[1]

Many children and young people say that their parents and teachers never discuss the nuclear threat. This is not all that surprising, given the potent fears—and feelings of grief, guilt, powerlessness—that lie below the surface. Yet lack of communication on this issue takes a high toll.

1. *Silence conveys fatalism.* It seems to say that our collective future is "not our business," that it lies in the hands of politicians and generals and experts who know best.

2. *Silence conveys indifference.* Amazed at how much those fifth graders knew about the nuclear threat, environmental dangers and world hunger, Global Education Associates asked them where they received their information. Did their parents and teachers talk about these problems? "Oh no," was the answer, "You see, grownups don't care." Adult silence on these issues not only appears as indifference, but as a lack of caring for the children themselves faced with a frightening future.

3. *Silence reinforces repression.* Grownups' difficulty in communicating in these areas teaches that certain feelings are taboo—feelings like grief, fear, anger at leaders, and compassion for those who suffer now and will suffer in the future. The Bomb becomes a mystery so powerful that it cannot be spoken. As a social worker from New York said, "It probably embarrassed my parents, and they sort of communicated that to me . . . Like sex, like death, like God, like certain things that happened in my parents' past they did not want to talk about."

4. *Silence breeds cynicism and anger.* Children and young people begin to wonder whether feelings of anguish over destruction and injustice even exist in grownups. If they suspect that they *do,* they feel contempt for our hypocrisy in pretending that everything is just fine. If young people conclude that such feelings do *not* exist, then the response is often one of rage. Their desire then is to shock our society awake, shake it into the realization of the impending horror. Punk rock, with its gruesome faces, ghastly costumes, grating sounds, is but one manifestation of this fury.

How do the young stand it? How can they keep their sanity? If I were very young, 16 or 17 years old, I think I would begin, perhaps very slowly and imperceptibly, to go crazy . . . If I were 16 or 17 years old and had to read or listen to that (U.S. Government reports on civil defense plans), I would want to give up on listening and reading. I would begin thinking up new kinds of sounds, different from any music heard before, and I would be twisting and turning to rid myself of human language. — Lewis Thomas, biologist.

And, of course, the toll is wider yet. The rising incidence of drug addiction, crime and suicide among teenagers and even children is sad evidence of the erosion of meaning. More pervasive still is a sense of alienation, both from family and future. This manifests not only in anti-social and self-destructive behaviors, but, less visibly, in the loss of the capacity to make meaningful choices and commitments. As a high school student said, "All that is left is to live for this exact moment, because we could go at any time."

As a parent I feel totally isolated in these feelings. My 14 year-old son feels guilty and inadequate when I cry while watching a news show. How do you tell a child what's ahead for him? How do you motivate yourself to try to live a better life? My friends say, "Don't worry; there's nothing you can do about it." — **Letter from Massachusetts**

What can we do to break the silence and meet our children on the level of their own deep responses? We parents and teachers can't make the world a safe place overnight. What in the meantime do children and young people need from us? Our communications with them will be easier if we know how we can be responsive and supportive.

1. *Know your own feelings.* As a parent or teacher, first identify and appreciate your own fear, anger and sorrow about what is happening to our world. While we want to be honest and open with our children, we don't want to use our conversations with them to explore or vent our own feelings. Attend a workshop or, using some of the methods in this book, organize a peer group where you can do this important work. In a group or alone, take time to talk to the child within yourself; feel his or her fears and hear through his/her ears what needs to be said.

2. *Invite children to share their feelings about the world.* To do that you can express your own in a gentle, uncharged fashion and encourage them to express theirs. Watching television you can say, "It makes me sad to see those weapons (fighting, poverty), how does it make you feel?" Explain why you are busy on the phone, making calls for a local peace meeting. "I'm working to stop the making of bombs, because I don't want to see a war happen. Do you ever think or dream about that?"

3. *Give your complete attention.* Once you have broached the subject, don't rush off on an errand and preoccupy yourself with another activity. Take time, even for silence. But don't force the issue. A child has the right *not* to hear or talk about nuclear war. Do not assume that he or she is oblivious or unconcerned, if at a given moment they are not ready to discuss it.

4. *Let yourself listen.* On this subject, says Kevin McVeigh, children have "a hunger to be heard." Accept the challenge not to interrupt them. Just in getting us to listen to them, they begin to overcome their sense of powerlessness and isolation. Physical contact is reassuring: "Come sit next to me, I'd like to hear about that."

5. *Help children define their feelings.* What remains unspoken and

unacknowledged is far more frightening than a danger we can see and label together. Many children do not know what they feel before they express it. Help them gain control over vague feelings by putting them into words.
gain control over vague feelings by putting them into words.

6. *Let them know they are not alone in these fears.* To know that you as parent or teacher have similar feelings about the world is more reassuring to them than if you pretend to be aloof and unperturbed. Tell them what you felt when you were little. "When I heard about Hiroshima, I was shocked and sad." "There were civil defense drills in school that made me scared." Share dreams you had, poems you wrote.

7. *Acknowledge what you don't know.* Children will ask questions you cannot answer. That is all right; it is nothing to be ashamed of; facts may not be needed. Remember that questions are often veiled statements about concerns and fears. Invite children to express the concern behind the question; the expression may help them more than any answer you can give. For example, "How are we going to get out of the city when the bombs come?" If you do not have a workable plan (and who does?), you can simply say, "Yes, I've wondered about that, too. What do you imagine might happen here? What feelings do you have about that?"

8. *Don't feel you must relieve your children of their painful feelings.* They are *their* feelings, and appropriate to the situation. You can clear up misconceptions that cause unnecessary distress ("No, Jimmy does not have a bomb in his house, and he can't start a war"), but anguish over the nuclear peril is a component of our experience in this time that cannot be taken or wished away. As parents we tend to want to do our children's worrying and suffering for them; but when we try to do that, we convey the message that we think our children are too weak to handle scary feelings. And to say "Now just don't worry about such things," teaches them repression and denial.

9. *Let children make choices.* Support them in making decisions about their activities and lives, to the extent they can do so without distress or harm. This helps them build their own sense of power. Express your respect for their copefulness.

10. *With your children, take joy in life.* Take time to watch a snail, talk to a star, plant some seeds, tend the sprouts. We are born with a capacity for wonder and children can help us recapture it. We in turn can convey our own sense of the sacredness and beauty of the web of life, sharing delights we have found in art and music, the inspiration we have drawn from stories of courage, and the treasures of our spiritual traditions. Second to our loving, supporting presence, these are the greatest gifts we can give our children in the nuclear age.

11. *Show them you care enough about your world and about them to engage in actions to avert disaster.* Children do not need a safe cocoon so much as a

community of shared beliefs and adventures. During the London blitz many children were evacuated to rural areas for safety. Psychologist Anna Freud compared their emotional responses with those children who stayed with their parents under the bombings, and she found greater psychic stability among the latter group. Similarly John Holt studied children undergoing the psychic stresses of the civil rights movements in the South amidst all the fear and occasional violence attendant on school desegregation. He found a higher level of emotional health among those whose families were actively engaged in the struggle, in spite of the dangers to which it exposed them. Vivienne Verdon-Roe tells of a second grade class where all but one of the children said they expected a nuclear war to occur. When the remaining child was asked why he was so confident of the future, he answered, "Because my mother and father go to meetings to stop nuclear war."

12. *Support children in taking action in their own right.* There is a great deal that they can do to work for peace and justice. They can write or draw a letter to the President. They can telephone the White House (202-456-7634); a courteous operator takes all messages. (One parent says, "We keep the number by the breakfast table; if there's something particular in the morning paper, we call, or maybe we just call anyway.") They can make posters and join rallies. They can volunteer at a local organization, stuffing envelopes, making calls, running errands. They can organize or join a children's action group, where they can discuss, learn, leaflet, march, and raise money for their cause in a variety of ways from lemonade stands to car washes. In addition to the impact such actions can have on the community, they do two important things for the youngsters themselves. They provide a strong and meaningful sense of peer support, so they no longer feel isolated and powerless with their fears for the world, and they enhance their sense of self-respect and self-esteem.

At an environmental meeting years ago, my young daughter Peggy and I learned that porpoises were being decimated by certain kinds of tuna fishing. Coming home we drew posters and leaflets; side by side we distributed them at the supermarket to discourage people from buying that kind of tuna. That action increased our respect for each other and our solidarity as a family. Since then we have engaged in many social actions together, and I think that one reason we don't "burn out" is because these actions are a way of experiencing and expressing our love for each other.

There are a number of methods for working with children in groups, which colleagues have found useful in helping them express their awareness of the dangers to our world and their feelings about them.

D/E Exercise 1
Group Discussion for High School Age
(30-60 Minutes)

When eliciting responses from a group or a class, begin with questions that are emotionally neutral and gradually progress to those that are more emotionally charged. As Eric Chivian suggests, the sequence could run like this:

— *How did you hear about nuclear weapons and the possibility of nuclear war?*

— *What did that make you think?*

— *How did that make you feel?*

— *How do these thoughts and feelings affect the way you see yourself and your future?*

D/E Exercise 2
Group Discussion for Elementary School Age
(1 Hour)

For children in elementary school the questions can be more frequent and directive, the pace livelier. The following format was used by Kevin McVeigh in a meeting with sixty sixth graders and their four teachers. He was introduced simply as an adult who is working to prevent nuclear war; asking the children to have paper and pencil at hand, he proceeded with a series of questions.

• *Can you remember a time when you felt very powerful? Close your eyes and make a slide show in your mind, with pictures of a time when you did something difficult or scary. Got a picture now?* (Show of hands indicates that everyone has a mental picture.) *Write a word or two on your paper to help you remember that time and that feeling of being powerful.* (He encourages a number of children to share their images with the group. After the questions there is sometimes just a show of hands, sometimes general sharing of responses.)

• *How many of you know about nuclear bombs and nuclear war?*

• *How many have talked with someone else about them? . . . at home with your families? . . . in class?*

- *Have you ever dreamed about nuclear war? Let's do another slide-show in our heads. Get a picture from your dream, or just have a picture right now about nuclear war. What do you see? Without opening your eyes, draw on the paper. It could be a picture, or maybe just some marks that express how you feel about what you see. You won't have to show this to anyone . . . . Now let's talk about that slideshow we just did . . . .*

- *What do you feel when you think about nuclear bombs and nuclear war?*

- *What things do you want to know about nuclear bombs and nuclear war?* (These are written up on the board for future reference.)

- *Do you wish that you knew more and that people would talk with you more about this?*

- *Now let's do another mental slideshow. Can you get a picture of something you really love about life or about the world? . . . Let's share some of those.* (e.g. "I saw myself in a little boat with my dog, and we were sailing along and I was real happy." Most answers by far were "my family.")

- *Go back to the picture of yourself being powerful (use the word or phrase you wrote down, if you need it). If you could feel powerful like that all the time, what would you do to stop a nuclear war from happening?*

- *What are some things you've already done? Has anyone ever written a letter to a public official?*

- *What are some more things people can do?*

As McVeigh reports, "I finished with a talk about fear and other feelings, and the power of individuals to change things. About the value of caring and acting. About the fact that lots of adults were working to prevent nuclear war. About what young people can do. About always remembering that you are powerful, and that anyone who tells you different is lying to you."

D/E Exercise 3
Team Drawings
(1 Hour)

Barbara Hegarty, who developed this activity, puts out crayons, rolls out long sheets of paper on the floor or tables, and invites the children to make two consecutive and composite pictures. She instructs them:

1. *Imagine that you are part of a civilization in danger of being annihilated in a nuclear war. This drawing you will make together is a message you can send to other civilizations on other planets. You can show the causes of this crisis so that other worlds will not let it happen to them.*

2. *Imagine that you are part of a civilization that has succeeded in dismantling its weapons and has become a peaceful, happy society. Now you are growing old, and in this drawing you want to communicate to future generations the dangers of weapons and the things you did to bring peace.*

D/E Exercise 4
Group Imagining
(30 Minutes to 3 Hours)

Hegarty also works with delinquent boys. She found them to be almost "totally disassociated from the rest of the world . . . and numbed to all feelings except hard, 'macho' anger. It is hard for them to see that anyone else in the world exists, let alone matters. So I've found that the most successful exercises involve imagining."

Giving them space to move about and lie down, sometimes out of doors, she invites them to imagine themselves as something else. They can start with a leaf, a drop of water, a cloud, a snowflake. As they "get into" this, they begin to imagine themselves as animals and then as other human beings on this planet, including those we take to be our "enemies." Giving them plenty of time, she encourages them to move, sing, draw what this feels like. They move into a feeling of interconnectedness with the rest of life. "It's all part of me, isn't it?" said a boy.

D/E Exercise 5
Folding Paper Cranes
(1 Hour)

Sadako was two in Hiroshima when the fire came out of the sky. Ten years later, as she lay dying in her hospital bed, she began to fold pieces of paper, for there is an old story of her people that if you fold a thousand paper cranes, your wish will be granted. Sadako and her family folded 966 paper cranes before she died. Now on the anniversary of the bombing, children come to her statue in the square and hang a thousand paper cranes. Strung like flowers, they express the prayer that bombs will never fall again.

In our country some people who work for peace fold paper cranes, too. Sarah Pirtle finds this activity a good way to talk with children about their hopes and fears for the world. Often she brings sheets of origami paper to a conference or meeting, and while the grownups are discussing the nuclear threat, she shows the children how to fold them. She tells them the story of Sadako, helping them to know how important and how beautiful is the work of bringing peace. And, as they finger the squares of bright-colored paper, the children begin to tell how frightened and sad they sometimes feel. "I'm afraid I'll be an orphan." "I'm afraid the whole world will blow up."

After feelings are shared, Sarah has them take each other's hands. Everyone holds on tight. "We are here with each other," she says. "When you have these thoughts and feelings, you don't have to be alone with them. You can find a parent or someone else who will listen. We all have these fears." And then they go back to folding paper cranes.

D / E Exercise 6
Roleplay of Telling a Younger Child
(15-20 Minutes)

This exercise grew out of McVeigh's work with the 6th graders (see Exercise 2). After the children had recalled and shared their feelings about nuclear bombs and nuclear war, they were asked, "How old were you when you first learned about them?" And the next question was, "When do you think that kids should first be told?"

At this point in the session the discussion became more focused, the mood more excited. The children were now the experts, the sources of wisdom. They unanimously agreed that six and seven years old was the best age, "and just tell them the exact truth."

This raised the question of *how* children should be told about the possibility of nuclear war. An eleven year-old volunteered to roleplay such a conversation with an imaginary younger child. He decided he would talk to his little sister, but then he got stuck — how to begin? The class decided that it is hard to offer this information "out of the blue" and that it helps to have some kind of question from a child first, like "What is nuclear?" or "Will a bomb fall here?" Given this opening, the boy proceeded to tell his little sister what he himself had wanted and needed to know at her age. "Don't tell *real* scary things, like that bombs could come in the night and kill everybody. Tell them that bombs aren't funny or things to play with." In discussing and enacting the process the children revealed a good deal of knowledge and also compassion for each other.

Again we see, and with children too, that it is our common felt responses to the dangers of this time that can instruct us and draw us together. Children know that it is a scary and dangerous world; they want us to acknowledge that fact and their feelings about it, rather than to try to shield them. When we meet them face to face with their deepest concerns, we find that it is we adults who gain. Clear-eyed, they can cut through our habitual defenses, our lethargy and statistical debates; they can summon us to wake up. Like those interviewed in the film "Growing Up Under the Shadow," children display an awesome degree of maturity in recognizing and describing the realities of the nuclear danger. In contrast, it is many adults who appear more "childish" with their fantasies that "it can't happen" and their evasions of responsibility.

Dear Mr. Regan:

I think that you should stop making any kind of bomb just because I am in 2nd grade does not mean I do not care because I do. In the world we have unuf bombs to blow up the world 10 TIMES! You miht think that I am just a stupid little girl but I am not. It is so discusting that there was going to be a war whith us, I woild take a knife and kill my self.

I am not the only one who cares. It is not funny at all! We want peace in our world! You might not no what happened in Japan in 1945, but I do and I an thousands of other people do not want it to happen agian any were I am going to tell my children about this. I am not being funny. I am not doing this because I head someone say that they did. There is a time to play and a time not to and I am not playing. I am Sarah Kerlin and I want this to stop.

— Letter from 7 year-old[2]

I have become increasingly aware that the question is not "what can we tell the children?" — but "what can the children tell us?" Sixteen year-old Sarah Rabin of the Vermont-based Children's Campaign for Nuclear Disarmament says that children feel a lot of distress and fear, but "I've never yet met a kid who doesn't believe we have a chance — if everyone of us works as hard as we can."

III

Relating in Counseling Settings

Certain professionals are placed in the positions of assisting people with their psychic and emotional burdens. The minister, priest or rabbi, psychotherapist or physician, social worker, teacher or counselor can be approached on a daily basis by people who are looking for help, comfort and guidance. Those of us who have selected these professional roles are confronted with human suffering and have assumed a certain responsibility to be with people while they describe their most intimate experiences of being alive.

The professional who works with people on this very personal level can choose to help them cope with the distress they feel for the world, as well as with their personal problems. It can be difficult, however, to move into those dimensions of concern, and many professionals have chosen not to do so. Many participants in my workshops have poured out feelings of pain for the world that they say they had never expressed to their therapist, priest or counselor. Let us look at the factors that discourage both counselors and clients from bringing such concerns into the work they do together.

Obstacles to Counseling About Concerns for the World

Lack of preparation. Professional training for most counseling roles focuses on the knowledge and skills needed for dealing with personal and interpersonal material. As psychotherapist Linda Monko puts it, "our professional training and theoretical foundations often do not prepare us for, nor support our interest, in dealing with global issues with clients."

Sense of professional limits. Society assigns the professional a role of being someone who has "all the answers" and can "make things all right." But, when a client raises feelings of distress over the condition of the world, we have neither answers nor cure. As psychotherapist Linda Monko observes, "The possible annihilation of our environment challenges the effectiveness of many popular methods of therapeutic treatment: medication may dull the client's awareness of his or her pain regarding this issue; behavior modification may help in diminishing feelings of anxiety; talking about how the client feels may bring relief through releasing emotions. But none of these remedies, which are focused on individual relief, will change the situation to which the client is responding." In this situation we confront limits to our healing skills; and it is hard to acknowledge those limits when neither we nor our clients want to hear about them.

Reluctance of the client. People come to us for help in dealing with personal problems, and they come with the assumption that we stand outside these problems and can offer a neutral and olympian view of them. It often simply does not occur to them to give attention to difficulties and feelings that we may share together, by virtue of living in the same world. Clients also fear that we will dismiss such concerns as irrelevant to their "real" problems, and as an avoidance of them.

Professionals' inexperience in dealing with their own distress. The client's expression of dread and grief over the condition of the world can put counselors in touch with their own emotional responses. Many of them have done little work on their feelings around these issues. A saying in the realm of psychotherapy is that "you can only take someone as far as you have gone yourself." As Monko explains: "When it comes to a feeling of distress for the world, we can be as affected as our clients. Not only are we faced with finding a way to cope with the issue ourselves, but we have the added burden of being asked to help others. When a client begins to grieve in expressing fear that her children may be separated from her 'when it happens,' that they may be painfully burned to death, it is difficult to avoid our own fear for our children. When a client begins to express anger because of his or her feelings of powerlessness to effect change of governmental policies, it is difficult to avoid our own sense of helplessness and anger."

Professional objectivity and distance. Monko goes on to say, "regardless of one's theoretical orientation, the ability to remain at a distance, to separate our clients' issues from our own, is a well recognized standard for therapeutic practice. However, the world is not just our clients' environment, but ours, also. Threat to the environment directly effects us all regardless of our professional credentials or role."

Notions about pathology. Professionals in medicine and psychology have traditionally been trained to look for disorders, and to interpret pain as a symptom of malfunctioning. Thus has pathology come to be understood. The original, literal meaning of pathology is *the study of suffering;* it held no connotation that suffering itself was wrong or sick. But over time, as psychiatrist Paul Dell points out, pathology has come to be seen as an evidence of malfunctioning. That makes it hard to recognize that some forms of suffering are normal and healthy. When a client experiences anguish over the condition of the world, the tendency is to suspect a morbid cause in their constitution or personal history — and to look for it.

I am a family therapist in a community health center, and I continually see the manifestations of despair in my clients. Worse than that, I see that those of us who are supposed to be helpers — well, actually the system through which we are supposed to deliver this help is broken, and I think it is broken and ineffective because of an unwillingness or an inability to acknowledge and confront despair, both personal and in the system as an entity. So that is where I am stuck.
— Workshop participant in Pennsylvania

Theories about the self. Western culture since the Renaissance has tended to view the individual as an independent, self-existent entity whose essential structure and dynamics can be understood apart from its context in nature and society. In the classical Freudian view its primary drives for sex and power set it in conflict with society and in competition with other beings. Such assumptions make it hard to credit that an individual can express distress on behalf of other beings, or the planet itself. In counseling about such issues as depression, drug abuse, suicide, career indecision and lack of commitment to long-term relationships, there is the temptation to consider the causes idiosyncratic, rather than imbedded in the social context.

I desperately want to talk about those fears; I couldn't because the group and the counselor would shoot back with, "and what do you get out of creating these worries? Do you use them as an excuse to drink?" . . . . I was encouraged to speak openly and freely about my family relationships — those were okay pains — but the others?NO. They were supposedly nothing more than symptoms of repressed personal issues.   — **Letter from Minnesota**

Considerations of faith. Our era puts a heavy burden on clergy, especially those engaged in pastoral counseling. In that role men and women seek to offer spiritual comfort and guidance, helping parishioners grow in faith and serving as models for that faith. Yet the unprecedented dimensions of global suffering and particularly the prospects of global destruction test that faith; they raise painful questions about the power and benevolence of God. While these questions can be addressed theologically, they are hard for the parishioner to face, let alone express. To acknowledge and share dread in the face of threats of mass annihilation is even more difficult for the pastors; for as shepherds of souls they are expected to deal with the anguish of others, not expose their own — to offer solace, not seem to seek it.

Suggestions for Counseling Relationships

As a counselor or as a client, make yourself aware of obstacles that stand in the way of using that relationship to deal with distress about the world and with problems that arise when that suffering is denied. Just the recognition and discussion of these obstacles helps move us beyond them. In addition, I offer alternative approaches suggested by colleagues and participants in despair and empowerment workshops.

Validate feelings of distress for the world. As counselors and therapists you have been trained to acknowledge and affirm a client's expression of feelings about self and personal relationships. In the same manner validate the feelings expressed about the condition of the world and the dangers of mass annihilation. The reality of these dangers makes it safe to assume that sorrow, fear, and anger about them are present at some level in each person. They are normal and healthy responses to the present situation and should be validated as such. Indeed, as the previous chapters stressed, these feelings of pain for the world are a testimony to a person's openness and compassion. As such they allow you to point out qualities that can enhance your client's self-esteem.

Encourage disclosure. Many clients, as we noted, expect counselors to be interested only in their "personal" problems and to treat feelings of global despair in a patronizing or reductionistic fashion — and therefore are not disposed to reveal them. Encourage disclosure of such feelings, especially in cases of depression and attempted suicide, as well as with problems in setting goals, making decisions and forming long-term commitments. Here a sense of futurelessness, even of impending catastrophe, is often at play. You can help clients get at it by asking if they ever worry about what might happen to their world. Lest the client think you are probing for neurotic preoccupations, you may need to volunteer some of our own anxieties about the world's prospects.

In eliciting their anticipations about the future, it is usually not enough to ask, "What do you see yourself doing in ten or twenty years?" People tend, in discussing their personal hopes and plans, to disassociate them from the larger context — social, economic, military or environmental — and to describe these plans or fantasies as they would unfold under normal circumstances. When they are invited, on the other hand, to describe what they expect the *world* to be like in ten or twenty years, their anticipations of loss and cataclysm are more likely to surface.

Countering fatalism. While validating the appropriateness of a client's feelings of anguish for the world and its future, you need, of course, to avoid appearing to collude with negative beliefs about the inevitability of disaster. Help the client see that the loss we all experience now is the loss of *certainty* that there will be a future, and not of the future itself. In that sense we are in a time of transition, learning how to live with our mortality as a species and expecting that challenge to evoke strong new qualities in each of us.

Similarly discourage the client from letting his anxiety or anger about the nuclear threat serve as a pretext for self-defeating behaviors. The Bomb is a given. We learn to live with it, integrating it into our awareness, the way we learn to live with past trauma — like abuse or rape — neither repressing it nor feeding on it as an alibi for self-pity or an excuse for self-hatred.

My experience indicates that the acknowledgement and exploration of a client's pain for the world will create little risk of incurring fatalism or obsession with doom. By its very nature and dynamics, especially when it is recognized as a measure of one's interconnectedness with the rest of humanity, its expression releases energy and enhances appreciation for life.

Encourage assertive response. It is appropriate to view clients' relationship to the present situation in terms of oppression. Certainly the threats of nuclear and environmental cataclysm inflict hardship, drastically impairing their sense of continuity and purpose in human existence, and fostering feelings of powerlessness. It is equally appropriate, therefore, to encourage clients to assert their right to be free of this oppression, and to regain control over their own lives. Rejecting the role of victim, they can assert their capacity to choose and to act. A variety of opportunities exist that enable clients to take action.

Reevaluate the counselor role. Far from being typecast as the fixer who "makes everything all right," or as the oracle who "has all the answers," the counselor emerges as a guide who accompanies. As guide, walk with clients, not only through their personal, family and professional difficulties, but also through their pain for the world and the darkness of our time — offering the reassurance of your presence and understanding, and the resources of your training and experience. In dealing with this global dimension of their suffering, do not let yourself get hooked into trying to solve the problem — because pain for the world is a given, unavoidable and incurable. Support clients as they wrestle with it, and help them discover in that engagement the dimensions of their compassion and courage.

Reevaluate the client role. When facing together the awesome threats of our time, the client also appears in a new perspective. Instead of a case to be solved or a person to be mended, he or she emerges as a fellow-journeyer, a gift, whose felt responses to a world in pain increases your own understanding of that world. As an open system, each conscious mind illumines a different arc in the loops and currents of knowing that interweave our world, each is another "neuron in the net," bringing distinctive perceptions and resources to our collective awareness. As we come increasingly to appreciate this, we find ways of conveying it to clients as well.

Family Work and the Nuclear Challenge
Carol Wolman, M.D.

The method I use is designed to help people look at and work through their blocks to communicating with their close relatives about their concerns for the world. The workshop should include 5-10 people who have at least 90 minutes to meet. The leader should have experience doing family-oriented therapy, and should have discussed his/her concern about the planet with some members of his/her own family.

Each person works individually for 5-10 minutes with some guidance from the leader and feedback from other group members. To start, she describes briefly the

the family situation in which she grew up — which parents were in the home, socio-economic status, and sibling position. She also describes her current relationships with parents, siblings, and other key figures.

She then chooses one relative and imagines how it would be to discuss her concern about the state of the planet and her work to prevent nuclear war [referred to below as "the work" — ed.] Gestalt and role-playing techniques can be used. The person works on her own blocks to communication — fear, anger, assumptions about the relative. The workshop leader must be alert to tendencies to blame the relative for the lack of communication, and redirect the person to her own inner process.

Each person completes her work by making a commitment to reach out to her relative in some way — in person, by phone, or by letter. If discussion with a relative has already begun, the person may decide to increase the stakes by asking the relative for financial or other support in doing the Work.

"A", a 35 year old man, hasn't discussed his concern about nuclear weapons with his father, because Dad is too old, sick, and rigid in his thinking. On exploration, "A" still sees himself as a little boy who is being bad when he confronts Dad with anything Dad doesn't want to hear. He decides to write Dad a letter about who he is and what his life is about, and ask Dad for his blessing for the Work.

"B", a 30 year old woman, feels that her twin sister is too straight and locked into the establishment to be open to "B's" work for peace. As she imagines the conversation, "B" realizes that she herself is being prejudiced and narrow-minded about her sister's life. She commits herself to asking her sister to be her partner in working for world peace.

"C", a 28 year old man, believes that his older brother, who works for an aerospace company, represents the U.S. military establishment. He comes to see that his "peace" work is partly a way of attacking his brother, and that his hostility is interfering with his effectiveness. He decided to send his brother some literature about the dangers of the arms race, and ask for feedback.

"D", a 40 year old man, thinks that his elderly Jewish parents are still terrified of his being politically active, because of their experiences with Nazism and McCarthyism. He realizes that times have changed, and that nuclear war is the primary issue now, and it is his responsibility to redefine what the crucial issues are. He decides to ask his parents for some money to help feed his family, since he is donating so much of his time to the Work.

"E", a 38 year old woman therapist, says that she has already tried to work out many issues with her family, and she has given up on getting through to them. She realizes that her sense of hopelessness about her family parallels her despair and inner paralysis about affecting the world situation. She commits herself to sharing this sense of hopelessness with her younger sister and asking for help with it.

This family work builds courage and confidence by forcing us to face our worst fears. It lends itself to long-term effort since our family ties are lifelong. In asking our relatives to help us with the Work, we define ourselves more and more clearly as people committed to bringing about peace on Earth in our lifetime. We overcome the tendency to see ourselves better or wiser than others. By testing our world view with the people who have known us longest, we keep ourselves honest.

Chapter Four

Despair and Empowerment Work in Groups

No matter how overwhelming the dangers that confront us may appear, none of us faces them alone. Our awareness and our feelings about the threats of mass annihilation are not private, but widely shared, because "we are in this together." In your communications with the people in your personal and professional life you can help them realize this in some of the ways we discussed in Chapter Three — and indeed some of you have been doing this already. The fact that our situation is a collective one, bearing equally on us all, has tremendous implications: it means that in facing it together openly and deeply we can rediscover our interconnectedness in the web of life, and this brings personal power and resilience.

This discovery has largely been made through working in groups. All the affirmations about interconnectedness, the web, and empowerment, which run through this book, derive from group experience. They can be *explained* in terms of systems theory, psychological theory, and spiritual teachings, but their truth for us who have engaged in the work comes from what we have *experienced together*. For in the last years thousands of people across the country and overseas have been gathering in churches, schools, retreat centers, and conferences in order to explore and share with each other their inner responses to the crises of our time.

Indeed it was only after many such groups that we could understand what was happening in them clearly enough to articulate their very purpose. Here is how we defined it at the national gathering of Interhelp in October 1982. The purpose of these groups is "to provide people the opportunity to experience and share with others their deepest responses to the dangers which threaten our planet — be they dangers of nuclear holocaust, environmental deterioration, or human oppression; and, in so doing, to enable them to know the power that comes from their interconnectedness with all life, so that they can move beyond numbness and powerlessness into action." This purpose, as we have learned, is best achieved in groups convened specifically for this work.

This chapter offers guidelines and suggestions for convening and facilitating such gatherings in your own community. It refers to this group work as *workshops*, and to what takes place in these workshops as the *work*.

I
Value of Working in Groups

Workshops provide focus and duration. In the daily run of life the global dangers facing us can appear both too remote and too horrible to discuss in a personal fashion without soon shifting the topic. But a workshop is like an island in time where, removed from other distractions and demands, we can focus together long enough to reach and explore our deep responses to these dangers. The group serves as a lens which helps us, as Chellis Glendinning puts it, "to sustain the gaze."

Group work provides support. The natural emotions evoked in us by the mounting threats of mass annihilation are hard to deal with alone. As many participants in this work have affirmed, "We need each other." We need each other to discover that our responses are not isolated, and that sharing them brings a deep sense of community and collective power. By its nature the workshop serves as a "safe haven" for exploring these responses together. As a naval commander in the Pentagon wrote, "The workshop provided a safe haven and highly relevant content, which for the first time allowed me to squarely face my feelings (about working with nuclear weapons) — without running. (It) resensitized a part of myself which had become numbed, and (I) take that pain as the basis for real spiritual growth and new directions in my life."

Workshops offer safe structures. They allow us to practice some behaviors that are uncommon in our daily social interactions. For example, we can hear each other's deepest feelings about this planet-time without assuming responsibility for these feelings or trying to mollify them. It gives us practice, furthermore, in expressing some of our own deepest dreads without trying to protect ourselves or others from them. In the process we discover how valuable these deep responses are in helping ourselves and each other to wake up to what we can do together.

Group work is synergistic. It reveals to us our own powers as well as our own feelings — our powers to give as well as to receive support and validaton. Dr. Robert Murphy, who does Despair and Empowerment work with groups of Vietnam veterans suffering delayed stress syndrome, attests to their ability to help each other deal with grief and guilt once these feelings are acknowledged and faced together. In so doing they discover unsuspected dimensions of their own sensitivity, generosity, and psychic courage.

Group work creates momentum. It provides a setting for initiating co-created endeavors. Participants in workshops often continue to meet afterwards, building support groups and undertaking joint actions.

II
Plotline of Group Work

When people meet together in a workshop what then do they find? They find a safe setting and structures which allow them to acknowledge and to explore their deep responses to planetary dangers. Breaking out of isolation and self-distrust, they experience the validity of these felt responses and find them to be rooted in caring and interconnectedness. This process suggests a plotline of the work in which a group engages.

This plotline, sometimes called the arc of the work, unfolds in three successive movements, as Joseph Havens, a veteran workshop guide, has delineated for us: despairwork, the turning, and empowerment. As we plan and conduct a workshop it is important that we attend to this dynamic flow — and sequence the group's activities in ways which invite it. Our awareness and our appreciation of this arc is more important than the particular methods we employ. Let's note these three movements:

1. *Despairwork*. Here, we evoke and consciously confront the realities of our planet-time — including the threat of nuclear war, the poisoning of our life support system, and the suffering of our fellow beings — and we acknowledge and experience, express and validate our felt responses to these realities.

2. *The Turning*. Here, the collective nature of our pain for our world is recognized as evidence of our interexistence, revealing the larger transpersonal context or matrix of our lives. As Glendinning puts it, "We allow the connection, we already have with all life to emerge into consciousness." Or as Havens puts it, "we re-weave the web." This is the turning point of group work where pain turns to power.

3. *Empowerment*. In the last section of the arc we then explore the kinds of power or synergy that are available to us as open systems. We do this on two levels, personal and social, or we could call them spiritual and pragmatic. In the first we explore ways of opening and deepening our perceptions of the resilient resources of the larger web. In the second, we apply these perceptions to our work for social change as we develop approaches, visions, and plans, so that each participant can emerge from the workshop able to take concrete and immediate steps.

The following chapters of exercises correspond to these movements. Let me acknowledge that it is somewhat artificial to distinguish them in any categorical way: the process is too fluid and dynamic to be put neatly into boxes. Despairwork alone is empowering. These elements of the plotline do not represent separate steps or categories of experience so much as an overlay of moments — one that indicates the direction of the work. It is not to be assumed, furthermore, that this tripartite movement: despair, turning, empowerment, is completed once and for all. It is a cycle that returns again and again as we move through the darkness of our time with its peril and its promise. Having traced its pattern in a workshop, we can then let it more easily recur in our lives, each time expanding our ability to respond — or response-ability.

The plotline does not need to be made explicit to participants in the workshop: be the judge as to whether this is appropriate. Some groups are reassured by a sense of overall structure and want to know that they won't "be stuck in despair." But to others this structure can impede their sense of spontaneity, and make the work seem contrived. So it is a question of art, of touch. Some sample agendas are included in Appendix A; you will detect the plotline in each.

III
Style, Roles and Skills in Guiding

To move through this process together, a group needs to be coordinated and guided. The group, itself, can share leadership by taking turns leading discussion and different exercises; one person can be the group guide; or a team of guides can plan and facilitate this together.

Each of us has his or her own style of working, as distinctive to us as the way we walk or laugh. Trust it. Our naturalness and genuineness in the work is our gift to workshop participants. If you are a singer, your workshop will probably draw heavily on the power of sound and music. Or if you are a dancer your participants will be encouraged to use their bodies to explore and express their responses to our world situation. Some guides, like myself, work within a fairly structured framework moving from one exercise to another. Others prefer a less directive approach, giving participants more leeway in setting their own agenda and following their needs as they arise.

We must remember that as guide we are not offering ourselves as experts or healers. We provide experiences and structures in which people can do their own work. We are there to facilitate this work, not to give answers or solve problems or cure.

The Roles of the Guide

So how do we facilitate? What is our role as guide? We have defined this role in the following ways and found them to be useful.

1. To design and provide structures and processes which invite participants to experience and to share their inner responses to the crises of our time, and also to experience the power that comes from our interconnectedness, in

order to act in the world with greater resilience; intentionality and creativity.

2. To present the goals of the workshop and to secure agreement on these goals. This includes the objective of each part of the agenda as well as the purpose of the work as a whole.

3. To create a safe setting, to help participants trust themselves and each other, by fostering a sense of permission, support, and community.

4. To keep the group focused on the purpose and the process, while being flexible and ready to change the agenda in response to the needs of the group.

5. To validate participants' feelings of distress for our world as normal and healthy, and to validate the unique contribution of each participant.

6. To help participants take responsibility for their own feelings as they arise and for the larger journey on which they are embarked as individuals and as part of a planet people.

7. To help participants see that these feelings and concerns are rooted in our interconnectedness.

8. To model this interconnectedness . . .
    — by a style of leadership that is serving not controlling.
    — by active, open listening
    — by trust in the process of the work, itself, without fear of heavy emotional responses.
    — by respecting peoples' defenses.
    — by encouraging people to co-facilitate each other's work.
    — by encouraging mutual appreciation.

9. To provide or encourage access to spiritual resources.

10. To help the group enjoy itself.

Skills of the Guide

To undertake such a multi-faceted role, what abilities do we need to possess or acquire? As I and my colleagues conducted more and more workshops, it became clear to us that a guide or facilitator should have or learn the following skills. You may find that many of these abilities are already present in you and need only clearer definition and practice. They are as follows:

1. To take leadership.

2. To articulate the premises and purpose of the work. (The premises are delineated at the beginning of Chapter Two; and the purpose of the work is restated in the introduction to this chapter.)

3. To set goals for a given workshop.

4. To design a multi-dimensional process by which these goals can be reached.

(The following four chapters offer a wide variety of methods to help us structure this kind of experience. And, of course, in addition you will draw from your own experiences and resources.)

5. To evaluate the workshop experience in terms of these goals.

6. To provide and conduct a variety of exercises to reach these goals, choosing the ones that are appropriate to the group, arranging them in any appropriate sequence and presenting and explaining them clearly and briefly.

7. To work within time limits. This means respecting the time constraints without pushing the group or appearing to be unduly controlling.

8. To describe your own experiences and feelings and to use them for the sake of the group — letting people know you, while judging the amount of self-disclosure that is appropriate to the group.

9. To help others share their own experiences and feelings.

10. To acknowledge and validate these sharings in a responsive, but firm manner (i.e. not trying to rescue people.)

11. To create a climate of safety through the choice of setting, through your own manner, and through trust-building exercises.

12. To set aside our own ego needs, personal agendas, and attachments to particular outcomes.

13. To give and receive feedback.

14. To observe the group responses and needs at each stage of the workshop.

15. To intervene in the process when necessary, judging when the group needs a change of pace, when it has gone off on a tangent and needs to refocus, or when one member is unduly inflicting his personal needs on the group.

16. To know our own limits and work within them.

17. To know the spiritual resources available to this work and to let them flow through us.

18. To be clear about why we undertake this work and the personal as well as planetary needs we meet in doing it.

19. To be willing to serve as a lightning rod for participants' fears, griefs, and angers about what is happening to their world and to view that role objectively with minimal anxiety and resentment.

20. To laugh at ourselves and to know joy in our interconnectedness.

IV
Emotional Levels of the Work

Despair and empowerment work can evoke powerful emotions: fear, anger, guilt, grief. This can be healthy and useful because emotions move us beyond numbness, release energy, and open us to our knowledge of what is happening to our world. In the "safe haven" of a workshop these emotions are often strongly expressed. There are two levels on which they can be evoked and addressed and it is important that the group guide distinguish between these. We recognize them as two forms the work can take: the *extensive* and the *intensive* forms.

The *extensive* form of the work is the most versatile and broadly used. While it lets emotions surface, it also lets participants feel fully in control of the expression of their feelings, and does not require that the facilitator be trained in emotional work. Most of the exercises in this book are of the extensive kind. The *intensive* form of the work is that which delves for powerful emotions and encourages their full discharge. Facilitators who are trained as psychotherapists, or who are experienced in such practices as Gestalt therapy, or Re-evaluation Counseling, sometimes use intensive methods in the despair section of their workshops.

Joseph Havens distinguishes these forms of the work in terms of the levels of defense they seek to overcome. Extensive methods move us beyond the resistance bred by social conventions and by our reluctance to face unpleasant facts and to experience unpleasant feelings. Intensive methods aim to overcome deeper defenses, those bred by fear of being overwhelmed by the intensity of our feelings and losing our moorings, or very sense of identity. It can be useful and growthful to break through these inner lines of defense but *only* if the facilitator has the appropriate training. If you lack such training, do not engage in intensive forms of the work; it would be both *dangerous* and *unnecessary*.

It is *dangerous* because if powerful emotions are released and you are unaccustomed to dealing with them in a trained and comfortable manner, both you and the participants will feel uneasy, possibly frightened. Instead of validating people's pain for the world, you can increase their fear of it. This has happened.

Intensive work is *unnecessary*, furthermore, because participants can get in touch with their deepest feelings without discharging them fully. Outward display is no measure of inner experience. This work is not therapy. Joanne Freer, herself a psychotherapist, says, "In this work, we do not confront people as a therapist, facing and focusing on their individual fears or personal histories, rather we walk side by side with them as we look together at the pain of our world."

And in the words of Frances Peavey: "It is dangerous, imperialistic even, to think that we activists or facilitators, are special and different, capable of greater understanding or spiritual depths than the others we affect. That is alienating, and untrue."

V
Dealing with Emotions

Even in extensive forms of the work powerful emotions come to the surface. Sometimes these are triggered by the simple sharing of information or the recounting of an incident; then feelings can well up that were controlled or denied earlier.

Most of us are unaccustomed to dealing with heavy emotions among relative strangers. How do we respond? Here are some helpful reminders.

1. *Be sure you have done a good measure of your own despairwork before attempting to facilitate others.* Only through experiencing such feelings firsthand, can you genuinely validate them in others as natural and normal, only then can you know them to be strengthening and integrating.

   If you have not allowed yourself to "touch bottom" in owning your pain for the world, you run two risks. One is fear of these apparently devastating emotions. The other is voyeurism. A guide who has not plumbed his or her despair feelings, risks using those of others as a vicarious outlet.

2. *Respect people's emotions.* As we have repeatedly stressed, anger, sorrow, fear and guilt are natural responses to the threatened loss of our world. Do not rush in to comfort when these responses well up. Your very presence, acceptance, and matter-of-fact bearing are reassurance enough.

   It is important to remember the distinction between our pain for the world and its emotional discharge. Tears indicate release of tension, they are healing. Laughter, too, is a form of discharge — and not to be taken as a sign of callousness.

3. *Respect people's defenses.* No one in the worshop should feel pressured to register or display emotion. Catharsis is healthy; but the outward expression of emotion is no measure of its inner intensity, or of a person's capacity to care. The stubborn stolidity of a person who is conditioned to control his feelings, can even be an asset we need in the saving of our world.

4. *Engage in the process.* Do not stay aloof from the flow of emotions. Participants are likely to feel inhibited and manipulated if you appear to be there as an observer or magus rather than as a full participant. In the workshop as on our endangered planet, we are "in this together." To express your own feelings as they arise, and to act simultaneously as guide, requires a split attention. This is tricky, but not as difficult as one would expect. Naturalness is the key. Like respect, it is available to us when we are on speaking terms with our own pain for the world.

5. *Trust the process.* It is not up to you as guide to resolve the emotions of the

workshop participants — or to rescue them by convincing them that "there is hope" or "life is worth living." If you fully realize that pain for our world is proof of our interconnectedness — that it can open us to the knowledge of the web of life — then you will not be shaken by expressions of despair. You can attend them with the tacit recognition that they are the birthpangs of the consciousness of our interexistence.

6. *Rely on the mutuality of the participants' experience.* Trust the compassionate community that arises in the workshop. As Bob Murphy attests in his despairwork with Vietnam veterans in Wyoming, and Barbara Hegarty in her despairwork with juvenile delinquents in Colorado, people are remarkably available to each other when they are dealing with a common anguish. As people recognize their shared plight — and behold each other expressing it openly — unsuspected reserves of caring and empathy are summoned forth. Keep your workshop open to the play of this mutual support, and expect that you will not give so much as you will receive.

VI
Personal Despair and Social Despair

"How does all this connect with my personal despair?"

"My anger over nuclear weapons — is it just simply my rage against the father who abused me?"

"How do I know if I'm weeping for the planet or my lost lover? (a lost child, a failed career?)

Such questions often surface in a workshop. Whether expressed or not, they are present in the minds of participants and need to be addressed.

As we have seen earlier, our culture, including mainstream Western psychology, is inclined to reduce our pain for the world to personal maladjustments. This kind of perspective leads people to suppose that feelings of personal despair must be resolved and eradicated before feelings of social despair can be considered legitimate. "First, I've got to work through my relationship with my mother . . . or with my addiction . . ." The notion that one must get enlightened, transformed, or one's head straight *first*, before dealing with social despair, keeps many otherwise intelligent people in a state of moral infantilism.

In any case, most people come to workshops with a good measure of personal as well as social causes of despair. They wonder about the relationship between the two and sometimes feel they cannot credit or validate their pain for the world, unless this relationship is clarified. In responding to this need I have found the following points to be helpful and true.

1. It is neither possible nor necessary to draw crystal-clear distinctions between the personal and social roots of our pain for the world.

2. Our experience of personal suffering can serve to sensitize us to the sufferings of our world. The poets and visionaries who saw into the nature of our time — the Kafkas and Orwells, the Kierkegaards and Virginia Woolfs — were hardly robust, "well-adjusted" specimens of mental health. They are like the ghost-trap, which Tibetan Buddhists weave of sticks and wool, and erect near funeral sites to catch wandering restless spirits. Some of us seem to be woven by life's fortunes to serve a similar purpose — to be ghost-traps catching the invisible currents of pain that haunt our planet-time. It is a useful function and permits us to give needed feedback.

3. Therefore, by virtue of our very infirmities, we can serve our world. Mahatma Gandhi, himself, was assailed by many inner, psychological contradictions, but he did not devote his life to their resolution on the personal level. As pscyho-historian Erik Erikson said, Gandhi was able to "lift his private patienthood to the level of the universal one, and to try to solve for all what he could not solve for himself alone."[1] This is the role of the "wounded healer." So can we, too, use our own hurts and failures to nourish our compassion — and action — for those who suffer now and those yet to be born.

4. At the same time the social dimension of our lives, including the global challenges we face, can inform — and even transform — the purely personal dimension. Elissa Melamed, a writer, therapist and workshop leader in the Interhelp network, stresses this. "Since we are integrative organisms, the impact of the planetary crisis is often combined with material from personal process . . . . For example, a woman with breast cancer found that her struggle for personal survival and her difficulty in contacting her own will to live was expressed as a pervading hopelessness about collective survival. Acknowledging this connection made her fight on both fronts more effective. Traumas in one's past can also play a significant role. A man whose sister died young let this event serve as a metaphor for his sense of grief about a possible cutting-off of future young lives. The sorting-out and integrating of these relationships between the individual and the collective, the past and the future is an important part of the empowerment process."[2]

If persons in the workshop need counseling or therapy in dealing with personal distress, encourage them to obtain it. Meanwhile the workshop's focus on the pain of our world will let them momentarily release their private preoccupations into the larger area of concern that they share with others.

VII
Stresses in Guiding Group Work

To guide a workshop can be profoundly rewarding. Such a privilege is not without its pressures—and it is well to recognize them. Some of these stresses are internal — such as feelings of fear and inadequacy to do the work — and some are generated externally through the reactions of workshop participants.

A sense of inadequacy can arise at the outset, as we present to others the nature and purpose of the workshop. It is a novel venture and can appear a bit threatening, especially when people feel resistance to facing their inner responses to planetary dangers. In speaking of the work we can, therefore, feel frustrated and misunderstood as peddlars of doom.

When the workshop takes place, the responses of the participants relieve these qualms. The release and empowerment they experience validate our efforts. Yet even so, if we continue to facilitate such groups, fears can assail us now and again. We may wonder what it may do to our lives, to serve as lightning rods for people's planetary anguish. The grief and horror they share in the workshops, from the depths of their being, stay in our awareness, fill us at times with a great sadness. Some nights, after a workshop, I have been haunted by the vivid images of apocalypse that people have felt free to share, and feel weighted with sorrow that such images shold impinge on their lives.

In addition to these burdens, a guide in this work experiences other pressures. People tend to be more demanding of the facilitator than in other kinds of workshops. Chellis Glendinning, who in the 1970's conducted hundreds of therapeutic workshops in holistic health, says: "People brought an open-ended attitude to those events. No matter how urgent their need, how profoundly or casually they engaged in the workshop, they were glad to gain some useful insight, information or approach. No one demanded that the workshop provide anything more than a step along the way. Workshops on the survival of our species are different. People often come feeling trapped, confused, desparate, and already know that no new therapy technique is going to save them. The demand on the workshop is often great and laden with emotions."

I, too, on occasion, have felt this demand about half-way through a full-day or weekend workshop. It is sometimes tinged with resentment — and, when it occurs, springs from subliminal, contradictory expectations of the guide. On the one hand, there is a wish for the guide to do something about the pain for the world that he or she triggered ("You invited me to feel it, here it is, now make it go away"); and on the other hand, there is the maddening recognition that no one can do that, for this pain is incurable; no one can "kiss it and make it well." It is not the pain itself, but a person's feelings about the pain — both fear of it and anger — that get projected onto the guide, much as a terminal patient projects his rage on the physician who diagnosed the disease.

How do we, then, deal with these stresses? When we embark on the work as a guide, we will find our own strengths. Here are some pointers in helping us to find them:

1. Have a support group where you can turn for encouragement and constructive criticism. This can be the group you trained with, or with whom you shared the theory and practice offered in this book.

2. Stay clear and grounded in your real intention. Remember why you are doing this work.

3. Remember that what participants said and did in a workshop is not a measure of its longterm effect on their lives.

4. Be patient with yourself and stay light. Play. Cry. Keep "breathing through" (Exercise in Chapter Eight).

5. Trust the interconnectedness of open systems. Let the knowledge of that web guide and sustain your work — like grace.

VIII
Getting People Together

The settings in which we can meet to engage in this group work are as varied as our lives. Workshops have been held in churches, schools, clinics, town halls, living rooms, in armories, and beside missile silos. They have varied in length from an hour and a half in the midst of a large urban conference to five days in a rural retreat. They can be held just once, or they can be a series where the group meets regularly over a period of time. They have ranged in size from a half-dozen people to one hundred and fifty or more participants.

To draw a group together, we can invite some friends and colleagues, or we can get a local group or organization to sponsor the workshop. The sponsor could be our church or temple, a peace group, civic organization, professional organization, or a particular conference.

In announcing the workshop, we want to state its focus as clearly as possible. Clarity is important because people aren't accustomed to meeting for this purpose. The announcement should not lead people to expect that the meeting is either to deliver and debate information or to plan strategies of action; rather it offers them the opportunity to explore their awareness of what it means to be alive in the nuclear age. See Appendix B for some examples of announcements that people have made for such gatherings and workshops.

The announcement can appear in local newspapers, newsletters, and bulletins. It can be verbally announced in church, on radio and television, at a meeting. It can be made into an attractive flyer or poster. The most effective means of publicity is often by word-of-mouth.

A time and a space should be set aside where participants can engage in the work without being distracted or interrupted by the demands of their daily lives. So you will want a space that can be closed to outside noise and disturbance, and preferably one that is spacious enough to permit people to move around and even to lie down. However, work has been done in cramped quarters like a crowded church basement where participants barely had room to stand or sit, or in noisy public settings such as a park or the corner of a high school cafeteria. Wherever the gathering place, remember that the real context or setting of the work is the threatened planet, our home.

IX
Preparing for the Workshop

I conducted scores of workshops before I had the sense to make a checklist that would help me and my colleagues to prepare easily, without confusion.

Stage One: Arranging the event.

☐ Clarify the purpose.

☐ Secure sponsorship of the workshop (an organization or church, a group of friends, yourself).

☐ Find appropriate space and time.

☐ Announce it (word-of-mouth, flyers, media).

☐ Specify what participants should bring (bag lunch, pillow, comfortable clothing . . .)

☐ Design the process.

☐ Distribute desired reading materials.

☐ Arrange needed carpools and childcare.

Stage Two: Physical Needs.

☐ Check the room for comfort, adequate space, light, heat, freedom from disturbance, access to parking, toilet facilities . . .

☐ Acquire needed supplies (newsprint, tape, markers, music, etc.)

☐ See that desired refreshments are available.

☐ Provide a sign-up sheet for names, addresses, phone numbers.

☐ Secure or prepare a list of local resources and organizations (so that participants can take appropriate action after the workshop).

Stage Three: Gearing Up.

☐ Review the design.

☐ Take moments to relax physically (brisk walk or stretching and deep breathing).

☐ Take moments to open mentally and spiritually to the wider purpose of the workshop within the context of people's lives and the needs of our planet.

X
Getting Started

The following five steps let us begin to guide people into the work they have come to do.

1. **Help participants to relax.** If people are new to the work, they usually come with mixed feelings and an initial measure of awkwardness and tension. A little body work helps ease these tensions, and lets people feel more alert and involved. Standing, stretching, and deep breathing can be done even in a large auditorium with rows of seats. Sound-making is excellent, too. (See D/E Exercise 7 in Chapter Five.)

2. **Help them to focus.** The workshop requires full attention and participation. Sit in a circle, if possible. Observers are a hindrance, so are coffee cups, note-taking, knitting, and other activities which tend to divert participants or cast them in an observer role.

   Take a moment to help people be mentally present. I often say: *We are here to use this time and space together. It is a unique opportunity. Our bodies are here, let us allow our minds to arrive also . . . . Many of us hurried to get here, perhaps leaving some chores undone and some calls we needed to make. Let's look at these bits of unfinished business in our mind's eye . . . and now let's put them up on a shelf, allowing them to stay there until five o'clock* (or whenever the workshop ends).

3. **Clarify the purpose of the workshop.** Make sure people understand that our

purpose here is to explore our inner responses to the condition of our world; it is *not* to discuss or debate the causes of this situation, nor to evaluate and plan actions we should take. This clarification, repeated at the outset, saves valuable time and energy.

4. **Affirm presence and power of feelings.** Acknowledge also from the outset, that these inner responses are inevitably charged with emotion. To feel grief, fear and anger is natural, indeed appropriate, and this is a safe place to express them. In this connection it is helpful to make the following three points:

   a. There is a difference between painful emotion and its discharge. A flow of tears, for example, does not mean that we are suddenly assailed by grief, so much as releasing the tension of that grief as it built up inside us.

   b. Discharge of emotional tension sometimes takes the form of laughter as well as tears.

   c. People have diverse emotional styles. Some can weep easily, others by conditioning and temperament, cannot. As Susan Wells tells her workshops, "There is no right amount to feel. We have different emotional conditioning and timing. We need our differences."

5. **Let people introduce themselves.** After your initial comments, which should be as brief as clarity allows — ten minutes should do it — let the participants begin to hear from each other. Even as they introduce themselves, they can move directly to a level of deep personal sharing; ways to let this happen are suggested in the section on Introductory Sharing (D/E Exercise 8) in the next chapter.

If the workshop is small enough (say under 25 or 30) these introductions can take place in the whole group, with participants speaking about a minute each.

XI
Building Group Energy and Participation

A good workshop is a highly participative venture; therein lies its power to connect, inform, invigorate. The greatest gift that the guide can offer to the participants is the opportunity for them to listen to themselves and each other. And when they really do that, so much caring and wisdom emerge that the participants themselves become co-facilitators in the work. Care should be taken, therefore, to help them stay open, alert, and engaged, and not slip into a passive spectator role. The following pointers can help:

1. *Verbal sharing in the group.* In a conversational discussion some individuals tend to dominate and some stay quiet, while others wait impatiently to get a

word in edgewise. This does not encourage full participation and attention. A "speaking object," which is passed around the circle or taken from the center by the person who wishes to talk, helps people take turns and slows the pace for better listening. Sarah Pirtle uses an African ritual wooded spoon in her workshops; Margaret Pavel uses a conchshell from the coast near her home; Bob Murphy has an eagle's feather which is passed from speaker to speaker; and I use a stone. Holding it gives weight and moment to the act of utterance, helping both speaker and listeners to focus more attentively to what is being expressed.

2. *Talking in small groups and pairs.* People can speak more fully, of course, when you divide them into small groups or pairs. By your suggestions, encourage them (a) to share the time and (b) to listen. Sometimes free conversation with lots of give and take is appropriate to the kind of sharing you want to see happen; but it can also be frustrating as it goes off on tangents, depriving people of equal time. Participants can express themselves more fully and at greater length if they do so in turns without interruption; this fosters better listening, too. If you choose that mode, it is helpful to tell the groups how much time is available (say five minutes per person), and to clap or ring when each interval has elapsed, or better yet have each group use a watch to time itself. (An effective, unobtrusive method for that: the watch is silently passed to the one who is speaking when his time is up, and then he holds it while the next person speaks, passing it to her after the allotted time, and she in turn does the same for the following one.)

3. *Nonverbal interactions.* Words, of course, are not the only form of communication and are, indeed, often inadequate to the deep knowings and feelings that arise as we face our pain for the world. What is there to be said right after people have looked over the brink or shared grief for their children, that does not risk sounding flat or trivial, or that does not dissipate the intensity of the moment? Sheer presence, steady, alert, and caring, can be the most appropriate response. Silent acknowledgement can be expressed through deliberate, sustained eye contact, as in *The Milling* (D/E Exercise 9) or the *Learning to See Each Other* meditations.

Imaging with colors on paper or with clay lets feelings and intuitions surface that lie below the level of words, and can serve to deepen communication between members of the group. So does touch, through the simple holding of a hand, or more fully and eloquently in *The Cradling* exercise. A loquacious and articulate engineer in Denver said, "The turning point for me was when I stopped talking and just looked, when I held that hand (in *The Cradling*) and realized — for the first time in my life — the sheer miraculousness of a human being."

4. *Checking-in.* As you guide you want to know what is happening with people in your workshop — are they bored? restless? do they feel frightened? or

isolated? You will want to check in with them now and again, and that is easy to do. When your intuition suggests that it is appropriate, just stop the proceedings and invite participants to report in a sentence what they are feeling at that moment about the group process. You can invite random comments or go around the circle systematically. Remember that you cannot meet everyone's needs at the same time and no one really expects you to, but the very act of checking in helps people feel more engaged and responsible. It can also prompt you to shift into another mode — to change the pace with a stretch, a song, a brainstorm, a small group sharing.

5. *Change the pace.* To keep up the group's energy it helps to vary the forms and pace of the work. I like to alternate between large group and small group sharing, and between verbal and nonverbal modes of exploration, and to intersperse them as well with moments for silent or guided personal reflections. Annie Prutzman takes time in her workshops for solo walks through the hills and woods near the conference center she uses. Kevin McVeigh has perfected the ten-minute "instant nap" — especially good after lunch. Let's not forget the invigoration of games. "Light and Livelies," as we call them, can take only two or three minutes and refresh the group. They are appropriate after the first section of the arc of the workshop and serve as a vehicle for the high spirits and even hilarity that can erupt after doing despairwork.

6. *Brainstorm.* Introducing the method of brainstorming to village organizers in Sri Lanka, I translated it as "thinking out loud together" and described it as "pretending we are one collective brain." Indeed, by its nature, it can let us feel that we *are* nerve cells interacting in a neural net. The process is familiar to many, but even so it is well to review the ground-rules, laid out in D/E Exercise 18 in Chapter Six, for they permit the process to be conducted in an invigorating fashion. I know of no method which is more consistently effective in eliciting the full participation of the group, raising its energy, and increasing its sense of commitment and creativity. It can be used to surface the reasons we repress our pain for the world, the difficulties we encounter in talking about it, the ways we have motivated ourselves and others to respond to the planetary crisis, the kinds of action we can undertake, the features of alternative futures we can build . . . . It is excellent for all ages.

7. *Buddy-System.* Sometimes, in workshops lasting over a day, I invite participants to establish a particular connection with one other member of the group. This is usually someone with whom they have happened to pair off in an early exercise. This buddy system, as the name suggests, works reciprocally: each looks out for the other and quietly checks in now and again. This can be useful. Given the potent emotional material we are dealing with, it helps to know that there is someone to whom we can talk when the need arises, without commanding the attention of the larger group, and to whom we are accountable for staying open and honest. It deepens the sense of mutual trust

and responsibility that a good workshop engenders.

8. *The touchstone.* As McVeigh points out, each of us has in our life an incident or image which seems to exemplify for us the horrors we face in our planet-time. It is usually the experience that broke through our defenses and caused us to take seriously the threats to our world. For him, it is his little sister's painful death from radiation-inflicted leukemia. For me, perhaps it is an old dream about my children in a nuclear war. For others it is a strip mine, or an oil-coated seagull stranded on the beach. These can become symbols, serving as touchstones to our deepest intentions to save our world. They ground us and fuel our commitment to work for change. To evoke these early on in the workshop, and perhaps refer to them again, keeps up the energy and momentum of the work — for they remind us of why we have come together and what we have, ultimately, to do.

9. *The Larger Circle.* By bringing to conscious awareness the sufferings of our time, group members gain a sense of participation not only in each other's lives but also in those of other beings. This larger context of the work can be made explicit quite simply and in a number of ways. For example, when people are standing or sitting in a circle, I often let them take a moment to imagine the vaster dimensions of the circle and all those whom it includes . . . an invisible circle linking us around the globe . . . . I let them close their eyes, take hands and feel that the hand they are holding could be that of a Russian soldier, or an American general or an Indian child (etc.) . . . often they speak aloud the names of those they invite into the circle, loved ones, our "enemies," government officials, military leaders, teachers who have gone before, and beings not yet born. Sometimes people bring into the circle endangered animals, a grove of trees.

XII
Closing the Workshop

A workshop where people have explored so deeply and personally deserves an appropriate conclusion. There are also matters of evaluation and follow-up to see to before people disperse. Allot adequate time as well for a closing circle, and end at the appointed hour, so that people with engagements do not leave before the others are finished.

Evaluation

Unless it is jarring to the group or unsuitable to the setting, provide participants the opportunity to give feedback on the workshop experience. (This is generally not appropriate to workshops of 2 or 3 hours.) Evaluation can be done in either individual written form or in a collective oral form.

If it is to be written, give the participants questions to answer (offering them either verbally or on a prepared form), such as "What did you find most valuable? . . . . least valuable?" Glendinning provides questionnaires for participants to mail back after a week. This has the advantage of allowing more time for reflection on the experience, and the chance to see its effect on one's life. It also has the disadvantage that some may be too busy to send the form in.

Evaluations done collectively and orally are quicker (five minutes can be sufficient). Done as enjoyable, high-energy brainstorms, they generate more items of response as participants' comments jog memories and trigger reactions. An effective form for this is three columns on newsprint or blackboard: above the first column draw a plus sign (for what participants especially liked), above the second a minus sign (for what they appreciated less or what did not "work" for them), and over the third an arrow (for suggestions for improvement). Often two or three sheets of newsprint will be needed as responses pour out. In true brainstorm fashion these are not to be argued, discussed or defended — just noted — and thus a rich blend of contrasting reactions often appears.

Participant evaluation of the workshop is important for several, fairly obvious reasons:

1. It provides invaluable feedback to you as guide letting you see the workshop through participants' eyes. It affirms strengths you may have doubted and indicates skill areas you will want to work on. Participant reactions are often different from what their behavior in the workshop might have suggested.

2. Your openness to this feedback is an inspiring example of light humility and unself-consciousness (of how people work in the "web").

3. Such evaluation offers participants an immediate opportunity to contribute to the work, building a sense of belonging and responsibility.

4. It also allows them a sense of completion in this particular workshop. They do not leave carrying reactions with them, like so much unfinished business.

5. When the brainstorm form is used, they can also hear and see the variety of responses and are less likely to generalize on their own.

Closing Circle

To reconnect a last time in a full circle gives visible, palpable expression to the mutuality we have experienced and the common goal we pursue. Speeches are unnecessary; if the work has been deep and potent, words chosen are mainly simple words of acknowledgement. As guide I like to acknowledge at that point, the inner journey we undertake as a planet people, the courage and caring of those in this circle, and the fact that the workshop is but one step in that journey. I remind participants that the deep responses uncovered here together are likely to well up in the days ahead more powerfully than ever before — for we have dropped our defenses — and that is all right, for we are strong and resilient and not alone. Even though this particular circle will not meet again physically, it will remain a part of our lives. I ask participants to take some moments of silence to look around the circle at each other, letting themselves be aware of what they learned from each and what they wish for each in the time ahead. After that silence, I invite a brief, random sharing . . . something they would like to say while we are still together physically. And then we end with a song, or sounding, or silence.

Other forms I use in closing a workshop are described in the empowerment rituals at the end of Chapter Seven. These structures allow freer and fuller personal responses. They are more suitable to a full-day or weekend workshop since they take longer, and presume greater exposure of the participants to the work and each other.

Follow-up

As we observed above in the closing circle, the workshop is but one part of a larger journey, a step along the way. Its meanings will remain more vivid and available to the participants if they can contact each other, continuing to draw on the mutual trust they built, the visions and plans they shared. Here are some ways to encourage this (some of the following have appeared on the workshop preparation check list mentioned earlier in this chapter).

1. **List of participants.** It is best to have people sign in, with addresses and phones, when they arrive. Make photocopies to be given out at the end of the workshop or sent later by mail.

2. **Subsequent scheduled session.** Annie Prutzman schedules an evening session, three or four days later, as part of the workshop; when people sign up they commit themselves to attend it. This, she says, has been highly successful, allowing participants to bring back some of the thoughts, plans, and experiences that were inspired by their work together.

3. **Information on local resources and action.** If you have collected materials about local opportunities, events, and organizations dealing with survival issues — or prepared a "menu" of them — make them available to participants. Point them out, but don't recruit. Put up a sheet where participants can write up further resources and actions with which they are familiar (this is preferable to their making a lot of announcements in the workshop).

4. **Mural of intentions and plans.** Many of the empowerment exercises (Chapter Seven) prompt participants to realize what they have to offer and to begin to make concrete plans for action. To let these be shared with the whole group enhances the commitment and momentum, and allows other participants to

offer their support. Since to share them verbally takes a long time, you may want to use a wall-chart (say a length of shelf-paper) on which people can write or draw them.

5. **Buddy check-ins.** If you have used the buddy system in your workshop, encourage each pair to call each other in the course of the coming week.

6. **Support groups.** A number of the participants may be ready to plan to reconnect with each other to form one or more ongoing support groups — or to create such groups with others in their lives. A support group can provide a regular checking-in, where this book can be used for further exploration and practice.

You may have little experience in guiding group work. I did not have much myself when I started conducting workshops. I made a lot of mistakes (and still do), often scolding myself afterwards for not having done it better. It would have helped me, I am sure, if I could have read this chapter three years ago, but it would not have helped as much as the experience of engaging in the process itself, of learning with people in the actual doing of the work. I invite you to allow yourself that experience.

The rest of the book offers tested methods for despair and empowerment work in groups, divided into chapters according to the plotline of the work. Try some of them if only with your family or friends. They and the guided meditations in the closing chapter may also be helpful to you as part of your personal journey.

Chapter Five

The First Stage Of
Despair And Empowerment Work

I would believe my pain. — Theodore Roethke

Zen poet Thich Nhat Hanh has said that what we need in our time is to "hear within us the sounds of the earth crying." In this first stage of despair and empowerment work that is what we do. We bring to awareness our deep inner responses to the condition of our world — to the threat of nuclear holocaust, the destruction of our environment, the suffering of our fellow beings. Blocked out by the pressure of daily affairs, they are now allowed to surface and are shared with others, as well. The methods offered in this chapter allow this to happen.

In this stage of the work we are dealing with both a psychological need and with defenses against it. "I am afraid for the world and I want to be able to talk about it," as a young man said in a workshop. Yet for many of us there is fear of expressing that fear, for to do so involves a dropping of defenses and the risk of appearing "weak". The work, therefore, requires a measure of courage, and of respect for those who undertake it.

To own and integrate this kind of pain for the world is a complex, but natural process that changes our relationship to it. The process involves, as we noted in Chapter Two:

- acknowledging this pain (verbally or silently).

- validating it as a wholesome response to the condition of our planet and the threats of annihilation.

- letting ourselves experience it.

- being able to express it to others.

- recognizing how widely it is shared by others.

- and recognizing as well that its source lies in our caring and interconnectedness.

In moving through this process, on our own or in a group, we can tap the deepest wellsprings of our powers to act. Then we reach that place where, as Thich Nhat Hanh puts it, "the pain and the joy are one" — restoring us to our inseparability with all life.

That inseparability manifests through compassion, which is what, in essence, we are dealing with here. Compassion means, as we have learned, to "suffer with." Despairwork methods reveal our capacity to "suffer with" our world — a capacity that is innate in each of us as open, interconnected systems. For we are not isolated, skin-encapsulated egos, so much as integral parts of a larger living whole, sustained by flows of matter, energy and information that extend far beyond the separate self. It is those interdependent flows which permitted the flowering of form and intelligence on our planet, and it is because of them that we now experience distress for our world — or "planetary anguish", as Blanc termed it. The extent to which we can experience that anguish is the extent to which we let ourselves be open to life beyond our skins.

We do not, therefore, have to instill compassion from without — telling ourselves or others what one "should" be feeling, if one is moral or noble. We only have to open to its presence within us already, as to an underground river flowing through our semiconsciousness, vital but perhaps unrecognized. There is no need to manipulate or force feelings; for to do so violates the integrity each can bring to our common enterprise. We can only help that river surface and flow together with the other streams that issue forth — into the light of day, currents mingling, gaining power and momentum.

D / E Exercise 7
Opening Out / Tuning In
(10-15 Minutes)

Most of us are braced, psychically and physically, against the signals of distress that continually barrage us in the news, in our cities, in our environment. As if to reduce their impact on us, and protect our sanity, we contract, like a turtle in a shell. Despairwork allows those tensions to ease. It is well, therefore, at the outset of a workshop, to turn to the breath, the body, the senses — for they can help us to relax, and open out and tune in to the wider, deeper currents of knowing and feeling.

OPENING THROUGH BREATH

The breath is a helpful friend in despair and empowerment work, and it is so in three ways: It connects the inside with the outside, manifesting our intimate reliance on the world around us. It connects as well the mind with the body; for lending attention to that everflowing stream of air quiets the mind, stills its chatter and evasions, let's us be more present to life. The breath reminds us, too, that we as open systems are ever in flow, not stuck within any given feeling or response, but dynamic and changing as we let it pass through us.

Breathe deep. Feel the air flow through the body like a blessing, the oxygen quickening each cell awake. Draw in that air that connects you with all being, for there is no one alive in this world now who is not breathing like you, in and out . . . who does not move with you in a vast exchange of energy with our environment, with seas and plants. Stretch high and wide to let more air in. Then fall forward from the waist with a forceful exhalation, expelling the tensions and poisons of the day. Let the breath cleanse, and open us.

As, in the course of the work, we let ourselves experience our pain for the world, the breath continues to serve us, much as it serves a woman in childbirth. It helps us stay loose and open to the knowings that need to happen and the changes that want to occur. The exercise called "Breathing Through," in Chapter Eight is very helpful.

OPENING THROUGH THE BODY

We turn also to the body, our faithful "Brother Ass" as St. Francis called it. All the threats facing us in this planet-time — be they toxic wastes, world hunger or nuclear war — come down, in the last analysis, to threats to the body. And our bodies have picked up signals that our minds may have refused to register; our unexpressed and unacknowledged dreads are often locked right there — in our muscles, throat or gut, and even in our ovaries and gonads too. It is well to check in with our physical connection to our planet and to our future.

Stretch. Stretch all muscles, and then release. Slowly rotate the head, easing the neck with all its nerve centers. Rotate the shoulders, releasing the burdens and tensions they carry. Behold your hand, feel the skin. Feel the textures of the world around you, clothing, arm of chair, tabletop. Your senses are real, they connect you with your world, they tell you what it is like. You can trust them.

In 1959 Lewis Mumford wrote: "In acquiescing to nuclear weapons, we have deliberately anesthetized the normal feelings, emotions, anxieties and hopes that alone could bring us to our senses."[1] Attending to our senses helps "bring us to our senses."

We met in the midst of a conference on the nuclear threat. The group was polite and dutifully attentive, though a bit tired after a morning of terrifying films, facts and figures. Before beginning our session I invited the people to breathe deeply, close their eyes and simply listen to their bodies. *We have been trying to handle this*

*information with our heads alone — as if we were a brain on the end of a stick —
now let's hear what our bodies have to say . . .* In the quiet that followed many
began to weep. And soon this group of relative strangers was sharing fears and sorrows they had seldom, if ever, expressed before.

OPENING THROUGH SOUND

To open up and tune in, we also turn to sound — sounds we make, sounds we
hear. The physical universe, say the ancient Hindus and modern physicists, is
woven of vibrations, and so are we. Releasing our attention into sound moves us
beyond the self's cramped quarters into wider apprehensions of reality. Nonmelodic
music can weave our awareness into those larger patterns. So, if not more, can
sounding — letting the air flow through us in open vowels, letting our voices interweave in *ah's* or *oh's,* in *Oms* or *Shaloms.*

This is a time to be still no longer, says theologian Harvey Cox. This is "a time
for crying out — as Hebrews cried out in bondage and Jesus on the cross . . . We
need to give vent to our massive pain and fear. A people must move from muteness
to outcry if they are ever going to take the next step." In sounding together we can
feel that outcry in our throats and bodies, feel it vibrate within and between us.

A few moments of sounding also clears the throat, helping us feel more present
to each other and ready to share.

OPENING THROUGH SILENCE

Many traditions, like the Quakers, know the power of "gathered silence,"
where together in stillness we attune to inner, deeper knowings. In this planet-time,
when we face dangers too great for the mind to embrace or words to convey, silence
serves. It can be as rich as sounding, while serving a complementary purpose:
sounding helps us to release the planetary anguish, silence helps us to listen to it.
This is important because no words are really adequate to express our response to
the possible approaching demise of our world. So, later in the workshop, once we
have had opportunities to specify our concerns and apprehensions, we take
moments to open into silence and meet each other there.

D / E Exercise 8
Introductory Sharing
*(30 Minutes for 25 People
or 10 Minutes for Groups of 4)*

A primary aim of a workshop is to uncover our deepest concerns about what is happening to our world. To this end participants need to hear both from each other and from themselves. This kind of sharing can begin right away with personal introductions.

The introductory sharing is concrete and brief (say a minute per person). Brevity has the virtue of letting everyone speak, of encouraging those who are initially shy, and of requiring the more verbose to distill their thoughts. Concreteness serves to make their sharing more potent, because it avoids rambling generalizations, and focuses on a particular personal experience.

TWO WAYS TO BEGIN

1. If time allows, it is effective to start on a positive note.

    As you tell your name and where you're from, tell us also something you love about this country (or this earth) Or . . . share something you did or saw today that made you glad to be alive.

To begin in an affirmative mode serves several functions: It provides a balance to the main thrust of the workshop. It reassures people that they will not be "pushed" into expressing feelings of despair. And, at the same time, it serves indirectly to bring such feelings closer to the surface. Barbara Hazard, a veteran facilitator who often begins with the question "What do you love about your country," says that it touches a deep nerve. "This question usually brings up a lot of feelings to the contrary as participants try to think of something. It is one of our deep griefs to have lost faith in the country we always loved (particularly for us middle-aged folks), and it is important to get back in touch with what we still believe in. It's part of reclaiming our pride in ourselves."

2. If time does not permit the above, we can move directly to the central issue: our personal responses to the plight of the world. It is important to get to this soon: Many people come to the worksohp just for the opportunity to express out loud and at last their feelings of apprehension without fear of being seen as morbid, sick or unpatriotic. To keep that initial sharing vivid, immediate and concrete, we can say:

    As you tell us your name, share an experience of the last week or so that caused you pain for the world. It can be an incident, a news item, a dream . . .

In inviting this sharing it can also be helpful to ask participants to observe the accompanying bodily sensations. Tuning to the body helps us listen to our inner experience and recapture the remembered incident, be it a child's nuclear nightmare or toxic leakage from a nearby dump.

"My name is Mark. I work on contract to the Navy, consulting on weapons systems. This week my little boy was sorting books for a school sale, and asked if he should keep some of his favorites to pass

*on to his own children. I could hardly answer because I realized that I
doubted whether he would live that long . . .*
— **Workshop participant in Maryland**

At the conclusion of this sharing, I point out to the participants that, in each
case, the deep concerns that they have just shared have a point in common: they extend beyond the separate ego, beyond our personal needs and wants. Whether expressed with fear, anger or grief, they are rooted in caring, and they are to be
honored as evidence of our interconnectedness. At this point I often introduce the
practice of "breathing through" (see Chapter Eight). It is useful to participants for
the rest of the workshop, as well as the rest of their lives, because it helps them to
handle pain in a way that grounds them in the realization of their interexistence.

TWO POINTERS:

1. Model the sharing first, even though participants know your name.

2. Before you do, allow some moments of silence. This allows participants to
   tune into their own experience, choose what they want to share; they then
   can listen more attentively to others.

NOTE: This kind of initial sharing can be very useful in other settings as well, such
as any meeting or classroom session on issues of collective concern. It engages people on a deep level, cuts through unnecessary verbiage and competition, and builds
solidarity. At the seminar at Notre Dame in 1978, which I described in Chapter One,
it was this simple exercise and its impact on us that allowed us to discover despairwork.

D / E Exercise 9

The Milling

(10 Minutes)

Just as the introductory sharing breaks the ice, so does the milling exercise — in
a nonverbal, and usually more intense and evocative fashion. It is good to use right
after the verbal sharing — or after the nuclear stories (Exercise 11). Instead of letting
the power of those shared images and experiences dissipate in a general discussion,
The Milling lets them sink in, while also allowing people to get up and move around.

Moving back chairs or cushions, participants are asked to mill — to circulate around the room at a fairly energetic pace. "Just pretend you're hired as extras in a movie about Times Square," I usually say. "Keep moving. No talking. Just circulate, pass each other." I model this, walking around the room, weaving through the people.

This exercise, which takes no more than ten minutes, has four or more parts; they are all nonverbal and participants usually need to be reminded not to talk.

1. In the initial "Times Square" milling, people are hurrying past each other as on a busy street.

2. *Now look at each other as you pass. Keep moving, but let your eyes engage. As they do, let yourself be aware that here is a person who shares with you this planet-time . . . . Now, as you pass a person, pause for a moment to take their right hand in yours. Be conscious of what this person has just expressed about their pain for our world. Just note that without speaking and pass on . . . .* This silent act permits a deep, respectful acknowledgement of what has previously been spoken. It permits people to *see* each other, openly, free from the necessity to say anything.

3. *Now put your left hand behind you, and as you pass a person try to touch their right hand with yours, without being touched back.* This is an abrupt change of pace and mood, inviting the participants to a childlike game, full of scuffles and laughter. Again, you will need to demonstrate this, because the shift to playfulness is unexpected. *There I got you! Touched your hand first. That's right. Quick now. See if you can touch without being touched back.* People begin to dodge and laugh. This moment of the exercise not only vents pent-up energies, but also reveals our simplicity: our "heavy" pain for the world is as normal and acceptable a part of our lives as a game of tag. We are in it together, with all our silly, human normalcies.

4. *"Okay. Now stop. Begin just circulating again amongst each other. As you pass a person now, take a moment to face them straight on. Put your raised hands together palm to palm, shoulder-height, and look into each other's eyes. As you do, let the possibility arise in your consciousness that this person may die in a nuclear war . . . . Just look, be open, don't speak . . . . Now move on. Face another, hands together . . . . Let the notion surface in you that this person may be the one you happen to be with when you die . . . ."* etc. for three or four such encounters. Some may weep at this time, some may hold each other, but keep your tone matter of fact: we are simply acknowledging the realities. This final part of the milling is a form of "death meditation." It confronts us with the transciency of human life, especially under the threat of nuclear war. Depending on the group and your own inclination, that threat can be made more explicit as people look at each other.

Many variations, of course, are possible. For example, it can be effective at a certain juncture during part two to have the participants close their eyes as they take a hand in theirs. This heightens sensory awareness, jolts the imagination. *Feel that hand in yours . . . it is still intact, whole . . . feel the life energy in it . . . explore it with your fingers as if you had never encountered a human hand . . . or as if it were the last you might ever touch . . . get to know its personality . . . is it timid? bold? would it be easy to push around? Test it . . . now get ready to say goodbye, let a final message be conveyed . . . slowly withdraw . . . .*

NOTE: Be sure, as the guide, that your comments are gentle and non-manipulative. Never tell or command people what to think, see or imagine, use language that is suggestive only, and is in keeping with present realities: nuclear war is a possibility, not a certainty. Do not say: "See this person before you as a victim of nuclear attack." Rather: "Let the possibility arise in your consciousness . . . allow, if you will, the notion to surface that this person may . . ." and the like.

Our workshops reveal that the reality of that threat breaks through our defenses with greater impact when we see it in the face and figure of another person — even a stranger. To confront their possible suffering or incineration seems to jolt our minds and hearts more than the imagination of our own death; it breaks open our capacity to care.

Since strong responses are evoked in the course of the milling, some facilitators like to permit participants to express them verbally at the end of the exercise. This can be done in twosomes, with people sitting down for a few minutes of "pair-sharing."

D / E Exercise 10

Open Sentences

(30 Minutes)

This exercise is also appropriate for the first stage of a workshop. It brings out in rapid, consecutive, verbal form each participant's felt responses to the condition of our world. It helps each to reflect on his or her habitual ways of dealing with them, while providing the opportunity to hear and be heard in a simple, thorough, nonthreatening fashion. It also offers a structure in which to practice listening with total receptivity. For many it constitutes a first opportunity to speak to certain issues without fear of comment or having to deal with rejoinders.

People sit in pairs, face to face, close enough to attend to each other without distractions, and refrain from speaking until the guided verbal exercise begins. The one in each dyad who is ready to go first is asked to signal this by tapping the other on the knee, and becomes Partner A. Partner A is instructed to repeat the unfinished sentences the guide will speak, and to complete them in addressing Partner B. Partner B is instructed to participate by saying nothing (stress this: *nothing*), and by listening as attentively and supportively as possible. Allow about a minute for the completion of each sentence; and give the participants warning each time before you begin a new sentence, by saying "all right" or "stop", so they can finish up in time to hear the next. The sentences I have found most useful are these nine in sequence:

1. *I think the chances of nuclear war are getting . . .*
2. *I think the condition of our environment is becoming . . .*
3. *When I think of the world we are going to leave for our children, it looks like . . .*
4. *One of my worst fears for the future is . . .*
5. *The feelings about all this, that I carry about with me, are . . .*
   (The syntax is awkward, but suggests the *ongoingness* of such feelings. We are asking people not what they feel at a given moment, but what they are conscious of carrying with them subliminally and continually).
6. *When I try to share these feelings with other people, what usually happens is . . .*
7. *The ways that I avoid expressing these feelings are . . .*
   (Keep that question in the plural; we only begin to guess at our patterns of avoidance).
8. *The ways that I avoid experiencing these feelings are . . .*
9. *The ways I can help other people deal with their feelings of pain for our world are . . .*

When the responses to these sentences are finished, invite A to express nonverbally his appreciation to Partner B for her support and presence; invite B to express nonverbally her respect for Partner A, for his courage in sharing in this fashion. Have them do this without speaking. Then reverse the roles, letting B complete the sentences while A listens.

NOTE: It is important that the listening partner not speak. What most of us most need is to hear ourselves say what is on our minds and hearts; and we are usually inhibited by the thought that we may appear to be asking for comfort or discussion. Note also the progression of these sentences. They move from views (what one observes to be occurring) to feelings (the midway and pivotal sentence) to our ways of dealing with these feelings.

This exercise permits many variations, of course: one can add or substitute sentences that reflect the particular nature or interest of the group. Guides of couples workshops have included sentences like: *If I am reluctant to share my pain for the world with my partner, it is because . . .* or *The effect of these feelings on my relationship with my partner is . . .* In workshops for parents and teachers, appropriate sentences can be: *If I hide my concerns for the future from the children, it is because I feel . . .* or *What I fear most in talking with the children about the nuclear issue is . . .* The essential factor is to keep the unfinished sentences as unbiased as possible, so that they can be relevant and useful to a broad range of experience.

D / E Exercise 11

Telling Our Nuclear Stories

(5-15 Minutes per person)

"Everyone has a tale to tell," writes Chellis Glendinning; "The total picture (of our nuclear age) includes the stories of each and every person who has lived in this era. How do we respond to the constant threat of death? How does living side by side with nuclear technology affect our sense of ourselves, our survival and our future as a species? After thirty-seven years honoring the taboo against speaking about nuclear weapons, *who have we become?* We know so little about ourselves in these times, and we will never understand until many, many people have spoken."[2]

Relating our nuclear stories is to break our silences, and bring to the surface the ways we have been living on an endangered planet. It is to perceive in the telling our inner cumulative response to the presence of the bomb, the slow poisoning of our environment, and the spread of hunger and exploitation. It is to tell it simply and concretely, from the first memory of hearing about Hiroshima, from the first moment we sensed as a child that something was going wrong—whether it was fish washed up on an oil-coated beach, a smog alert, a park strewn with cans and bottles, or civil defense drills in school that pretended we could survive a nuclear war. It is to "come out of the closet" at last, honoring the hidden currents of planetary anguish that have threaded through our years and days.

Glendinning describes a retreat where eight of us shared our nuclear histories, "sitting around a fire, sipping tea and story-telling, one by one. The first night one man said: 'Telling our stories is like passing the pipe. It's like an initiation rite. In a metaphorical way, we are passing around the circle and going new places together.'"

"An initiation rite into the Nuclear Age," as Glendinning calls this story-telling, allows us to perceive new contexts of meaning and to begin to create our own sacred history in this time. Symbolic dimensions emerge. "We might see the nuclear scientists — Einstein, Teller, Oppenheimer, Fermi, Szilard and the others — as god-like men who used their power of mind to meddle with the mysteries of matter and energy. The journey to the underworld was taken by the victims and survivors of Hiroshima and Nagasaki, by American servicemen who were sent to 'clean up' the bombed cities, by atomic veterans ordered to witness testing in Nevada and the South Pacific, by the inhabitants of the islands where testing took place, by Native American uranium miners and the residents of Harrisburg. Each and every human being on the planet who has grappled, consciously or unconsciously, with the uncertainty of living in the nuclear age becomes the hero."[3]

How do we create a setting for telling our stories? Glendinning offers guidelines:

- *The first step is to find people who would like to share their stories in a supportive way. You might start with the group closest to you: family, church, political organization, circle of friends. I have encouraged nuclear storytelling in many situations: in buses, conferences, university classrooms, cafes, dinner parties, with individuals, with groups.*

- *The person or group needs to agree on focus and ways of sharing. The focus is to share experiences and feelings about living in the nuclear age. Ways of sharing may vary. If members of the group are accustomed to expressing deep feelings, they may want to cry or hit pillows as part of the telling. Or they may prefer to sit in straight-backed chairs and talk. They may want to go to a special quiet place, or simply do it on their lunch-hour at work.*

- *Sitting in a circle is wise. As the tales come forth and we face their content and the feelings they elicit, we need the support that a circle seems to provide.*

- *The stories themselves are an intertwining of events, feelings and thoughts. Some important questions to cover are: What are my earliest memories of nuclear weapons? What is this history of my awareness? When has it been greatest? When least? What important emotional experiences relate to nuclear weapons? How do I numb myself against their reality? How do I cope with what I know?*

To these guidelines I would add the following, which I have found helpful in initiating nuclear story-telling in workshops:

- I like to make it explicit that these stories relate to the full gamut of our pain for the world, that is, not only to the nuclear threat *per se*, but also to environmental destruction and the spread of human oppression, which some feel yet more acutely.

- In a workshop setting I specify that each story will be told without discussion. No need to respond or comment, only listen.

- Time limits help give everyone an opportunity, and are not experienced as restrictive if made clear beforehand. Depending on the size of the group and the time available, I break the workshop into smaller circles, letting each participant take five to ten minutes. A few moments of general silence before beginning, allows each to bring her or his story to mind, so that each can then listen to the others without distraction.

Dr. Robert Murphy describes in a letter his own experience with nuclear story-telling in his local peace group in Wyomng. "During our first evening I passed a bright-colored three-inch feather to the first person in the circle, who was to "tell her own nuclear story" and pass it to the next person when she had finished. Anyone who wished not to speak could just hold the feather for a while in silence, which would include us all. None did. By the end of the ceremony at least half of us had stumbled upon unanticipated memories and feelings that made us weep, men as well as women. The charge of energy that filled the room after the ensuing discussion was electric, and both community talks and letters to the editor have been flying since."

D / E Exercise 12

Life Trajectory

(15 Minutes)

This exercise is useful near the beginning of a workshop to surface repressed anxieties and conflicting expectations about the future. Elissa Melamed, who developed and used it in Europe, reports that it was highly evocative, *and* provacative in what it revealed.

She begins with a guided meditation to help participants relax and look back over the course of their life in the context of world events. Each then takes pencil and paper and draws a line to represent that journey from birth to the present. On that line each records the major social and personal events that shaped their life. That in itself gives a fresh appreciation of our personal history, since we seldom pause or allow ourselves the distance to take so sweeping a view of it. After the participants have done that, Elissa then asks them to turn the paper over and continue the line from the present moment until their death. They are to note the anticipated date of their death and the major events they expect to happen in the future. At the close they discuss in small groups.

The most striking feature of the experience, she reports, is that many people found they had a "schizophrenic" view of their future. They would write in a normal death date, say at age 75, then often, on second thought, make a cataclysmic break midway down the line, say at age 41. They made comments such as this: "I first put down 75 because that is what I always thought I'd live to . . . but now I realize I don't expect to live to be old at all . . ."

D/E Exercise 13
The Cradling
(20-60 Minutes)

A form of guided meditation on the body, the cradling exercise, serves several purposes: It permits deep relaxation, which is all the more welcome after dealing straight on with frightening issues. It builds trust, and a kind of respectful intimacy between participants. It widens awareness of what is at stake as we face the dangers of the nuclear age. At the same time it taps deeper levels of knowing, breeding respect for life and recognition of the powers that are innate in us.

It does all this by focusing on the body — which is appropriate enough since our nuclear anxieties and fears for our collective future have ultimately to do with that. Dangers of fall-out and famine, of environmental collapse and genetic mutation, of nuclear blast, burn and radiation — all come down, after all, to their effects on the physical embodiment that we are and that we share. Usually, in contemplating these dangers, we try to get our *minds* around them; we deal with them on the informational level, as if we were brains on the end of a stick. The cradling exercise offers us the occasion to still our chattering, defensive minds and to listen to the wisdom of our physicality. For many participants it is the most memorable part of the workshop..

Depending on the time and space available, it can take two forms: the shorter one takes from 10 to 20 minutes; the fuller version, lasting about 45 to 60 minutes, is described here in the way I usually conduct it.

The participants work in pairs, Partners A and Partners B. Partners A, removing shoes and glasses, loosening ties and belts, lie down on the floor, close their eyes and relax. I help them do so by offering a brief guided relaxation (stretching, lying heavy, feeling the breath, relaxing toes, feet, legs, etc., moving awareness gently up through the whole body to release all tensions). I also model how Partners B will attend to them: lifting and cradling legs, arms and head in turn. B will do this in accordance with the verbal cues I then proceed to give. Soft nonmelodic background music, like flute sound, is helpful, but not necessary; carpet is nice, too; but even when done on a hard linoleum classroom floor, in the midst of a busy conference, this exercise can be profoundly effective.

Two key dimensions of the experience are these: (1) On the sensory level, the participants experience being physically supported and cared for. After having acknowledged and shared their pain for the world, they can now let it and themselves be held, as in the vaster web of life. To the same extent they have in turn the experience of giving support, of ministering to the other. (2) On the psychological level, the exercise enhances awareness — indeed permits rediscovery — of certain qualities of life, as it takes form in us. Here the verbal cues of the facilitator are important, quietly calling attention to the uniqueness of the human body, its long evolutionary history, its organic complexity and beauty, its vulnerability . . .

A matter-of-fact tone is appropriate. Few participants have opened themselves to such an experience; respect them for their trust and stay ordinary, avoiding a charged, portentious or sugary tone. Allowing appropriate pauses of silence, remain casual and reflective, as if observing some constellation in the heavens or a conch shell on the beach.

Lift gently your partner's arm and hand . . . . Cradle it, feel the weight of it . . . flexing the elbow and wrist, note how the joints are hinged to permit variety of movement . . . . Look, look as if you had never seen it before, as if you were a visitor from another world . . . . Observe the articulation of bone and muscle . . . . Turning the palm and fingers, note the extraordinary intricacy of their inner structure . . . . What you now hold is an object unique in our cosmos: it is a human hand of planet Earth . . . . In the primordial seas where once we swam, that hand was a fin — as it was again in its mother's womb . . . . Feel the energy and intelligence in that hand — that fruit of a long evolutionary journey, of efforts to swim, to push, to climb, to grasp . . . . Note the opposable thumb, how clever and adept it is . . . good for grasping a tool, a pen, a gun . . . . Open your awareness to the journey it has made in this lifetime . . . how it opened like a flower when it emerged from the birth canal . . . how it reached out to explore and to do . . . . That hand learned to hold a spoon . . . to tie shoelaces. . . to throw a ball . . . to write its name . . . to give pleasure . . . to wipe tears . . . . There is nothing like it in all the universe.

Gently laying down that hand, move now to your partner's leg and slowly lift it . . . . Feel its weight, its sturdiness . . . . This species stands upright . . . . Bend the knee, the ankle, note the articulation of bone and muscle. It allows this being to walk, run, climb . . . . Holding the foot, feel the sole, no hoof or heavy padding . . . . It is this being's contact with the Earth . . . . Feel that heel; when it kicked in the womb, that was what the parents first felt through the wall of the belly . . . . "See: there's its heel" . . . . And such journeys that leg has been on since then . . . learning to take a step and then another . . . walking and falling and getting up again . . . then running, climbing, kicking a ball, pedaling a bike . . . a lot of adventures in that leg . . . and a lot of places it has taken your partner . . . into work places and sanctuaries, mountainsides and city streets . . . gotten tired . . . sore . . . still kept going . . . . Gently putting it down now, move around to the other leg and cradle that one, too.

Observe this companion leg and foot . . . which shared those journeys . . . and many yet to come . . . . For all its weight and sturdiness, it can be broken, crushed . . . no armor. . . just skin that can tear and burn, bones that can fracture . . . . As you hold that leg, open your thought to all the places it will take your partner in the future . . . into places of suffering perhaps . . . of conflict and challenge . . . on missions that your partner doesn't even know about yet . . . to serve, to guide . . . . As you lay it back down, let your hands express your wishes for its strength and wholeness, that it may serve your partner faithfully.

Lift now your partner's other hand and arm . . . . Observe the subtle differences from its twin on the other side . . . . This hand is unique, different from all other human hands . . . . Turning it in yours, feel the life in it . . . . And note also its vulnerability . . . no shell encases it, for those fingertips, that palm, are instruments for sensing and knowing our world, as well as for doing . . . . Flexible, fragile hand, so easy to crush or burn . . . . Be aware of how much you want it to stay whole, intact, in the time that is coming . . . . It has tasks to do, that your partner can't even guess at . . . reaching out to people in confusion and distress, helping, comforting, showing the way . . . . This hand may be the one that holds you in the moments of your own dying, giving you water or a last touch of reassurance . . . . With gratitude for its existence, put it gently down; move now around behind your partner's head . . . .

Placing a hand under the neck and another beneath the skull, slowly, gently lift your partner's head . . . . (Partner A keep your neck relaxed, let your head be taken, heavy, loose) . . . . Lift that head carefully, cradle it with reverence, for what you now hold in your two hands is the most intricate, complex object in the universe . . . a human head of planet Earth . . . a hundred billion neurons firing in there . . . vast potential for intelligence . . . only a portion has been tapped of that capacity to see, to know, to vision, create . . . .

Your hands holding your partner's head — that is the first touch he or she knew in this life, coming out of the birthcanal into hands, like yours, of a doctor or midwife . . . . Now within that skull is a whole world of experience, learning, thoughts, memories, scenes and songs, beloved faces . . . some are gone now, but they live still in the mansions of that mind . . . . It is a world of experience that is totally unique and that can never be fully shared . . . . In that head too are dreams of what could be, visions that could shape our world and guide us . . . .

Closing your eyes for a moment, feel the weight of that head in your hands. It could be the head of a Russian soldier or an Indian farmer, of an American general or a Chinese doctor . . . . It is each of us . . . .

Looking down at it now, open your awareness to what this head may have to behold in the times that come . . . to the choices it will make . . . to the courage and endurance it will need . . . . Let your hands, of their own intelligence, express their desire that all be well with that head . . . . Perhaps there is something that you want your partner to keep in mind — something you want them not to forget in times of stress or anguish . . . . If there is, you can quietly tell them now, as you lay their head back down . . . .

Allow time for the recumbent partner to stretch, look around, slowly sit up. Then A and B reverse roles, and the verbal cues are offered again with new variations. At the conclusion of the whole process, time to re-orient is important — for the participants have journeyed into reaches of experience far from ordinary modes of interaction and need a quiet interval for return. It is useful then for the pairs to gather in foursomes to reflect together, sharing what emerged for them from this experience.

The example of verbal guiding that I wrote out here is not offered to be followed verbatim, only to illustrate the kinds of cues that are evocative and appropriate to the work. Each facilitator has their own style in leading this exercise, their own knowings to draw from. But whatever the language or images used, it is wise to touch on certain themes. Interweaving through the spoken words, these motifs renew and sharpen awareness of what it means to be a living person. They include:

1) the uniqueness of the human species in the cosmos.

2) its long evolutionary journey.

3) the uniqueness of each individual, and of each personal history.

4) the intricacy and beauty of the human organism.

5) its universality, linking us to other humans around the globe.

6) and its vulnerability.

In the context woven by these themes, the act of holding and observing is as potent as being cradled. Indeed the two halves of the process are complementary, letting us experience in both the active and passive mode the wonder and fragility of life as it takes form in us.

Note that if the number of workshop participants is uneven, it is best for the guide to pair up with the extra person, so that no one is left out. Then lead the exercise while acting as Partner B, simultaneously speaking and doing the cradling — but then not reversing roles.

When participants lie down remember to have them so place themselves that there is adequate room for their partners to move around them to cradle arms, legs and head.

If there is not enough floorspace for half the participants to lie down, a brief version of the exercise can be conducted as they sit facing each other. This also can be done if time is insufficient for the longer form. In that case, the exercise focuses on the hands, arms, shoulders, neck and head. Since the head, in the sitting position, cannot be really cradled, have the partners direct their attention and touch to the shoulders and neck (with awareness of the stress they hold, the kinds of burdens and tensions they carry, etc.), and then gently hold and rock that head in their hands. For that, if space permits, they can move around to hold the head from the rear. If this is impossible or too awkward, don't worry. So long as there is touch and attention, even the briefest form of this exercise is evocative and powerful.

In the crowded auditorium of a conference on the hazards of nuclear war, I asked members of the audience to take the hand of the person next to them, to hold it for a moment, and look at it. Then, as above, I offered reflections on what they held and saw. It took three minutes, yet out of a whole day's worth of speeches, panels and films, that is what many people remembered most vividly; for some it was a turning point. In this time of abstractions and information overload, the simple reality of touch, of embodiment, can break through our numbed defenses.

D/E Exercise 14
Imaging with Colors or Clay
(30-40 Minutes)

PURPOSE

The verbal expression of our concerns for the world has its limits, for words can hide as well as reveal. We are all conditioned to use language not only to communicate, but also to protect ourselves, to distract others' and our own attention from what is painful or embarrassing. We engage in discussion, analysis, debate — sometimes to clarify issues, and sometimes to obscure and dodge their impact on us. To connect and release our deepest responses to the condition of our world, it is useful, therefore, to go beyond words — or dive beneath them — to that subliminal level where we sense the threats to the preservation of our species, and register inchoately the anguish of our time. On that level we can tap our energy and the springs of our creativity. Images give us access to that level. They offer a doorway through which we can enter the realm of our intuitive responses to the nature of our planet-time.

When we use colors on paper, or model with clay, images surface; the tactile, visual engagement releases them, wordlessly. According to neuro-psychologists, it shifts the locus of mental activity into the right hemisphere of the brain. It is there that we find the capacity to think spatially, rather than consecutively, and to open our awareness to the web of life. Workshop participants are often surprised or startled to behold what their hands have portrayed: potencies of feeling and reaches of concern that they had supposed were peripheral to their lives. Unlike the words we speak, these images seem to have a reality of their own: we feel less need to apologize, explain, or defend. The images, once birthed, are just there — like a fact of life, self-existent — and viewing them we feel at the same time both revealed and protected.

STEPS FOR THE GUIDE

1. **Offer materials and adequate workspace (floor, tabletops).**

2. **Explain purpose.**

2. **Acknowledge people's hesitations.** Many people, especially adults, feel dismay when asked to engage in any form of artwork. Make clear that the point here is not to portray or create anything, so much as simply to let responses arise in us through our hands.

4. **Encourage them to work in silence.** To let these responses arise, we need to let our thinking, talking minds take a rest. You may choose to put on some appropriate music.

5. **Set time limits and inform them of the amount of time that is available.**

6. **Suggest themes for the imaging.** I sometimes put up on the wall three phrases: nuclear war, environmental destruction, human oppression — and invite participants to let images emerge in response to any or all of these. Ba Stopha and Joan Bokaer in Ithaca have developed a process that lets the themes arise from the workshop itself. Offering felt markers and rolling out a long sheet of newsprint on the floor, they invite participants to write in silence single words or phrases denoting the conditions in the world that cause them distress. Three or four minutes suffice, and then the sheet is taped to the wall. Maintaining silence, the participants look at all the words and phrases, and find one that speaks to them with particular impact. Then each works alone with smaller individual sheets.

7. **Suggest modes of work:** You can choose to have people use either their dominant or nondominant hand. The experiences are very different, each has its rewards. Working with the nondominant hand frees us more completely from the control of the censoring mind and our fears of being judged. It keeps the focus on color and movement alone and on the feelings they release. The dominant hand permits people to express forcefully and without frustration, the images that have arisen. For dominant hand drawing allow more time (say 15-20 minutes), for people become very engrossed.

8. **Offer a brief preliminary period for relaxation and centering.** Joseph Havens tells his workshops, "Take your time. Just gaze at the paper and see what images arise. If you feel stuck, you can write a phrase or two to prime the pump . . . . As you begin to draw, watch the changes that emerge, be open to new directions, go with them . . . if a whole new set of images comes and you want more room, turn the page over, take another sheet . . . "

9. **Allow time at the end for quiet discussion.** Imaging work is incomplete without the opportunity to share and explore it together. Have people gather in small groups or the larger circle, their drawings face down. Then one by

one they can turn their sheets over and verbally describe what they saw and felt as the lines and colors emerged on the paper. Gentle questions and observations from other participants can deepen discovery of what the drawings reveal and let them speak to each of us. Sometimes different drawings seem to resonate together, complete each other. At the close people often like to tape the sheets to the walls and take time moving about looking at them, commenting, absorbing.

VARIATION

Another form of imaging together is to have participants co-create a team drawing — on a long roll of newsprint on the floor or the wall. This can be suitable with intergenerational gatherings, where adults and children can each — in turn or simultaneously — draw something that makes them "feel sad about the world." To do this first and in silence, and only later tell about what they have put up, encourages the children to express themselves in the company of grown ups. They feel readier then to share what is on their minds, especially since they are freer with color and images than many adults.

COMMENT

The power of this kind of exercise in a despair and empowerment workshop was evident the first time I did it. One of the participants was Bill, a businessman active in progressive politics. In the introductory sharings as people expressed their feelings of pain for the world, he was impatient and judgmental; he chided people for indulging in "negative thinking," said such feelings of "doom and gloom" were weakening and that he for one saw no grounds for despair. Those reactions of his continued so long as our interactions remained on the verbal level. Then Joe Havens lead an imaging exercise, and we worked in silence with colors on paper. Bill sat for a long time just looking at the blank sheet in front of him; only in the last minutes of the agreed quarterhour did he take a felt marker and draw. As we gathered in small groups he displayed his drawing; it was very simple: a circle with longitudinal and latitudinal lines, with blue around it. In that circle, our planet, was suspended a large human tear. "That is the sadness," he said quietly. "The sadness I go to bed with every night and the sadness I wake up with every morning. The sadness that we have wrecked our world and that it is too late to save it, the sadness that my kids are just out to make money and get their kicks and don't seem to give a damn . . . "

In his small group a woman, a local peace worker, had drawn a picture of a nuclear power plant — stick figures encircling the cooling towers showed how protesters could close it down; and off to the side a group of kneeling figures showed, as she explained, the spiritual resources we need for strength and courage if we are to take action to save our world. Studying her images, Bill said after a moment, "Prayers and protesters aren't enough. Not enough to get us going, to keep us out there. We need the tear, too." And he pushed his paper over next to hers.

CLAYWORK

I have referred mainly to imaging on paper, because in a workshop it is easier to arrange and less messy than modeling with clay. Yet claywork, being more tactile and involving larger muscles, evokes deeper responses than drawing. Experiences, alone and with groups, have shown me what a potent means it can provide: both for releasing emotion and tapping our subconscious wisdom. To illustrate this, I can share a personal experience, as I described it in an article on despairwork. It occurred on a spring weekend during the Vietnam war when, despite involvement in a number of large-scale protest actions, I felt sapped by a sense of futility.

"To give form to feeling, and tired of words, I worked with clay. As I descended into the sorrow within me, I shaped that descent in the block of clay — cliffs and escarpments plunging into abysses, dropping off into downward-twisting gullies, down, down. Though I wept as I pushed at the clay with fingers and fists, it felt good to have my sense of hopelessness become palpable, visible. The twisted, plummeting clay landscape was like a silent scream, and also like a dare accepted in bitter defiance, the dare to descend into empty nothingness.

Feeling spent and empty, the work done, my mind turned to go, but then noted what my fingers had, of themselves, begun to explore. Snaking and pushing up the clay cliffs were roots. As they came in focus, I saw how they joined, tough and tenacious, feeding each other in an upsurge of ascent. The very journey downward into my despair had shaped these roots, which now thrust upward, unbidden and resilient. For long moments I traced them, wonderingly, with eyes and fingers."

D/E Exercise 15
I AM A ROCK
(10-15 Minutes)

Most of the methods described in this section seek to evoke repressed feelings of pain for our world by encouraging us to believe that such feelings exist in us. It is their operating assumption that on a deep inner level we are responsive to the distress of our time, and that compassion — the capacity to "suffer with" — inheres in our nature. If that is all we acknowledge, the despairwork can be incomplete and even partially blocked — for it is not the whole story. We have other responses, too, to the state of our world — disinterest, indifference, unconcern, sometimes even callous contempt and resentful rejection of the sufferings of others whether they are living now or in future generations. That such responses are present in us is evident in the life-styles we continue to maintain, and in the use of our time and money.

To weep and wail in workshops over social, military and ecological conditions can be a profound release, but it can also cause some participants to feel a bit hypocritical. "If I care so damn much, why haven't I done more about it?" Or, if some find that they are not even feeling the pain or compassion that others are expressing, their own sense of numbing or inadequacy can intensify. "The despair *I* feel," said Tom, a university student in a New York workshop, "is that I don't feel despair. My heart feels like a rock. I'm afraid I don't care, the way the rest of you do."

It took courage for Tom to say that, and in doing so he helped us. In the large circle we sat with his words: "I don't care." "I am a rock." I reflected aloud on the fact that in a way he spoke for us all. In each of us, alongside whatever else we feel, are dull indifferences and disengagements, desires to shut out and shut down. "Let's get in touch with them, for they are there and we know them. Let's just say them out loud, with all the vehemence that's in them. 'I don't care.' 'I really don't give a - - -,'" 'Leave me alone.' Let's feel that in our body, too, see how it feels in our muscles, in our gut."

That brief impromptu exercise, which took only a few minutes, released a lot of energy in the room, and people were eager to share what it meant for them. One woman, a college counsellor who had suffered through the holocaust in Europe, had been among the most expressive of her feelings of grief and compassion for the world. Now with some surprise, she said, "When I shouted out 'I don't care,' my first reaction was great relief. I think I've wanted to say that for a long time. It felt wonderful. I am free not to care, to be a rock!" Her face was brighter than at any previous moment of the day, her gestures larger. She wasn't finished: "Then, as you said, I felt what my body was doing — it was contracting like a sea urchin, prickly and closed in on itself — like this. So now I know I can do that. But it is not comfortable, and it would get a little boring."

In the work that followed, Tom was more present than he had been before and experienced, perhaps, the deeper feelings of connection with our world that he had "despaired" of finding.

Since then other ways have emerged to help people acknowledge and move through the feelings of hard indifference that we all carry within us. In pairs, participants can take turns telling each other how much they don't care about what is happening to the world. They tell why they don't care and what it feels like not to care.

D/E Exercise 16
Despair Ritual
(1-2 Hours)

Originally developed by Chellis Glendining shortly after the Three Mile Island nuclear plant accident, this ritual allows the spontaneous expression of our deepest feelings and knowings about what is happening to our world and our future.

It is an *intensive* form of the work and should only be guided by a trained person. It is described here because many (though not all) participants have found it to be the most significant and revealing part of the workshop. It reveals to them the unsuspected depths of their anguish for the world, and how the release of these powerful, shared emotions brings an equally powerful sense of community, courage and commitment. As such the ritual, when used, serves as axis of the workshop. I offer it only in a weekend workshop or, on occasion, a full-day one; for it requires time — not only to let the process unfold, but to build trust beforehand and to digest it afterwards.

The ritual draws elements from two different traditions: (1) It derives its *form* from the Native American circle, which represents the integrated "whole" of tribe and cosmos. (2) Its *content* was inspired by the practice of "speaking bitterness," which was used to alleviate the apathy and paralysis of the peasants in post-revolutionary China.

People confessed, not their sins, but their sorrows. This had the effect of creating emotional solidarity. For when people poured out their sorrows to each other, they realized they were all together on the same sad voyage through life, and from recognition of this they drew closer to one another, achieved common sentiments, took sustenance and hope.[4]

In the despair ritual, action takes place in three concentric circles. At the outset everyone is standing or moving in the outer ring, which is the Circle of Reporting. The next is the Circle of Anger and Fear, and the innermost is the Circle of Sorrow.

Before we begin I remind people that the distinctive character of ritual, which makes it different from other forms of interaction, is that it allows us to speak archetypally. Removed from our ordinary roles and identities we can give voice to those knowings and feelings which press to be uttered through us. Sometimes these knowings and feelings seem to be clearly our own, but sometimes they are not — and we find ourselves speaking on behalf of others and even of our planet itself. The anger we express and the tears we shed are then not just our own, they may be the rage of a Vietnam veteran or of an Indian mother — or of others of us in this very ritual. Since some of us have been conditioned to repress our emotions, we can recognize that others, who are socialized to be freer with their feelings, express them for us — and we can recognize our solidarity with their feelings by standing or kneeling beside them.

The ritual begins as participants begin spontaneously to report what is on their minds and hearts about the condition of our world. They state information or feelings — simply, briefly, without explanation. "I hate smog," or "Energy companies in the Southwest gave tailings from uranium mining to Native Americans to build homes and schools, and they didn't say the material was radioactive," or "I am afraid my children will die in a nuclear war." After each such statement the group as a whole responds by repeating "Indeed, it is so." This outer circle provides us with the experience of saying out loud, publicly, the facts and figures we usually sweep under the rug — and of hearing them, not denied or rationalized, but boldly acknowledged, confirmed. Sometimes a statement is made with which others may not agree, such as "There is no hope for us," or "Weapon makers are mad." In that case we still say "Indeed it is so," because that is what the person is genuinely feeling at the moment — and the ritual is a place for expression not argument.

When emotion wells up and participants feel moved not just to report but also to express it, they move — randomly and at their own choice — into one of the two inner circles. In the intermediary circle they stride, stomp, pound pillows, scream out their anger or fear. Or they move directly to the innermost Circle of Sorrow, where pillows are piled, there to release their grief by weeping, huddling or holding each other.

The great advantage of the three circle form is that it permits people to participate together at different levels of emotional engagement and catharsis. Highly dynamic, it allows them to experience the fluidity as well as the depth of their feelings, as they move back and forth between the three circles. The outer, encompassing one provides a safe place to wait and watch, while still contributing a supporting presence.

After negative feelings have been expressed at length, and may have reached a crescendo, the tone and direction of the group often shifts. The movement *down* into the darkness and pain begins to turn of its own dynamic into a movement *up* toward affirmation, as people experience the profound commonality of their responses — and the caring and compassion from which these responses arise. Statements like "My father, a veteran, is dying of cancer" are replaced or interspersed with "I am planting a garden," "We are building a solar house," "Our neighborhood is organizing a cooperative store." This development is not programmed or inevitable, but it usually occurs. It has occurred in all but one of the thirty or so rituals I have conducted at the time of this writing. Sometimes the shift or turning is expressed in spontaneous song and embraces; and then the ritual can begin to close. If it does not, that is because participants need to stay longer with their feelings of despair. Even then the mood begins to shift: the participants' expressions of feelings become gentler, imbued with compassion for each other. As the energy starts to subside and one can sense some temporary kind of completion, it is appropriate to begin to close the ritual.

In that case, whether or not the group as a whole has begun to express affirmation and hope in the future, the guide then moves to close the ritual by acknowledging the significance of what has been shared, letting people honor each other for their participation. At this point I engage participants in some activity that helps them refocus on the group as a whole. Taking hands we can move about, sounding or chanting, so that each person can face every other in respectful acknowledgement. Or, if we find ourselves on the floor in the center, we may begin massaging each other's backs. Many spontaneous songs have generated from this closing moment of the ritual, as well as some fine silliness. It is the kind of high hilarity that can surface when deep emotions have been released and deep solidarity is felt.

Some pointers to the guide, or, as Glendinning calls him or her, the "roadperson":

1. *Participate.* Don't hold aloof from the ritual. But participate with a split attention, for it is your job to give preliminary instructions, set the tone, provide safety and permission, and to watch for moments when you may need to intervene. It takes a lot of psychic energy; be sure that you trust your access to that energy.

2. *Intervene if people "reporting" from the Circle of Reporting fall into dialogue or debate.* This should not be necessary if you have clarified the distinctive nature of ritual.

3. *You may choose also to intervene or provide support to people undergoing extremely heavy emotional discharge.* You can do this by touch or simple physical presence beside them. Reminding yourself — and also the persons — that they have a choice about the extent to which they experience and express their emotions.

4. *In introducing the ritual re-emphasize the fact that everyone has different emotional styles and timing.* Each is valuable; no one should feel pressured to behave in a particular way.

5. *Some people, by their conditioning or temperament, will hold back from full participation.* Let them know, by words, gestures, eye contact, that they are still an integral part of the process.

6. *If nothing seems to be happening, just breathe deep and wait.* Stay with it. Let people take their time.

7. *Place the ritual in the middle of the day, and schedule a break to follow it.* People need time to absorb the experience, and brief rest period following. It

is not good, or likely, that people will separate and go home immediately afterwards. They need each others' quietly affirming presence.

COMMENT

Each time I guide this ritual I have trepidations beforehand, fearing that people will not engage in it, and each time, in a different way, it deepens and enriches the group experience. The time I felt the most reluctant to offer it was in a workshop in Boston where my two college-age children showed up. I feared that we would inhibit each other. I feared that, if we didn't inhibit each other, they would discover the extent of my pain for their future. I also was afraid of embarrassing them. I realized how much easier it was to guide the ritual with strangers than with my own family. Indeed, my anxiety was so great that I fell on the way to the workshop, tore a ligament in my hand, and had to lead the workshop with my arm in a sling.

The ritual took place — and acquired its own momentum, letting each participant express his or her full range of feelings and knowings about the planetary crisis. Such is the nature of ritual — and the safety it provides — my children seemed to forget my presence or at least were not inhibited by it. I witnessed with anguish and respect the dimensions of their awareness of what is happening to our world. I saw my son's unbridled grief over the poisoning of our environment, saw him dive into the pillows in the Circle of Sorrow and sob there over toxic wastes and the loss of animal species. I saw my daughter's fury over the violations of women: "There's a woman raped every nine minutes!" she screamed in the Circle of Anger and Fear. And both of them heard what I had not wanted them to hear — the extent of my dread over what may befall them.

A year and a half later I was in New York for the people's march in connection with the United Nations Special Session on Disarmament in June 1982; and my son, who meanwhile had graduated from college and taken a job working on toxic wastes in Massachusetts, joined me. He came along to the workshop I was offering the next day at Columbia University. "Are you going to do the ritual?" he asked. "No," I said, "there isn't time for it in the workshop." "But that is the most important part," he said.

Chapter Six

The Second Stage: The Turning

The shared exploration of our deepest fears and longings about our Earth has in it the seeds of a profound spiritual renewal. It draws upon the riches of existing traditions, yet is solidly grounded in the fresh love and faith born of opening our deepest selves to one another. Come join us in this widening circle. — Joseph Havens

Despairwork allows us to look full-face at what is happening to our world — the destruction and suffering that is wasting our planet and threatening the future of life itself. It opens us as well to the anguish attendant on that knowledge, to feelings of dread, anger, guilt, and grief. As we break through the taboos that have caused us to repress them, we can perceive the distinctive character of these feelings: we find that the dread is not the same as the fear of our own personal death; that the anger is anger on behalf of others as well as ourselves. We find a guilt that is not personal blame, but a kind of collective culpability, as a society and even a species. And underneath them all, on the deepest level, there is sorrow — a great sadness over what we are permitting to happen. We encounter dimensions of feeling that extend far beyond the personal ego with its separate needs and wants.

There comes a point, in other words, when we can realize that our feelings of pain for the world arise from our essential interconnectedness, that they are intrinsic to the web of life itself. The very distress that had seemed to isolate us from people around us, now manifests as part of the connective tissue in which we cohere — revealing us to be not isolated atoms, but cells of one living body. This realization, whether it comes in a flash of insight or a gradual dawning of recognition, is a turning point which changes our perceptions — or, more precisely the way we interpret our perceptions. It changes the way we see ourselves and the way we understand our power.

I
Names and Images for the Turning

For individuals this turning point arrives in different ways, at different times; often it occurs again and again, each time at a deeper level of our consciousness. But when we are working as a group we make it part of the collective process, finding the appropriate moment to pause and name and experience it together. In a workshop, this moment is usually about halfway through. At that point we turn the corner.

To describe this *turning*, as we have experienced it in countless workshops, I find myself reaching for metaphors. It is like a shifting of the tide, or the pause between breathing in and breathing out. Having drawn in and gone deep with the pain of the world, there is that pause of meaningful impact, of chemical change, before our heightened energies and insight are released into the world in action. Or it is like a fulcrum, which lets us shift the weight of our social despair, which lets us turn and raise it into a new way of being. The Chinese character for crisis is combined of two forms: one means danger, the other opportunity. On this fulcrum danger turns to opportunity.

Or it is like a hinge. Having opened to our pain for the world, we have found the hinge by which we can open also to our power for the world. This hinge can swing us from pain to power because it is anchored in their common source: our interconnectedness in the web of life.

Or, another metaphor, it is a gateway. Like many an ancient temple, its approach is guarded by demons and gargoyles. In facing them down, in moving through our dreads and griefs for the world, we gain entry into the truth that awaits us. We break through to new ground. There we discover our "deep ecology."

One of the basic norms of deep ecology is that . . . with maturity, human beings will experience joy when other life forms experience joy, and sorrow when other life forms experience sorrow."
— Arne Naess, Norwegian Scientist

Once breaking through to that ground, we see that our pain for the world is the "good news" of a larger consciousness at work. It is the universe knowing itself through us.

This awareness comes like a kind of grace. As meditation teacher Stephen Levine says, "grace is a sense of interconnectedness . . . it is the experience of our underlying nature, then we may see that what is often called tragedy holds the seeds of grace. We see that grace is not always pleasant, though it seems always to take us to something essential in ourself."

This shift in perception is an inner revolution that religious traditions call *metanoia* — turning around. From a spiritual perspective we "turn around" into wider awareness of who and what we are — as members in the body of Christ, or jewels in the Net of Indra, as the beloved of Krishna or neurons in the mind of God. It profoundly alters our notions of what is possible, and of the resources on which we can draw for the healing of our world.

"How do you program this?" You can't. It is in no way the doing of the guide — it is a function of the psychological and spiritual dynamics of the work itself, thanks to the systemic nature of life. As in every other aspect of the work, the guide simply offers people ways of acknowledging what they are already discovering to be true.

What, then, do you as guide need to do? You are helping the group turn a corner. At a corner you can look two ways, getting a fresh perspective on where you have been walking — and glimpsing, at the same time, a new vista. Looking back at what the group has experienced in doing despairwork, you *name* the interconnectedness that is intrinsic to their pain for the world. All the concerns they have experienced extend beyond their individual needs and wants, and point to the fact of our interexistence. As a guide you register this fact each time, with fresh appreciation. Point it out to the group with all the awe and affirmation it elicits from you. Looking ahead, as the corner is turned, you indicate what this interconnectedness can mean for them in taking action to heal our world.

> *Jerry, as you wept for your children's future . . . Jan, as you opened to the grief and confusion of your clients . . . Bill, the rage you feel over the dumping of toxic wastes . . . Helen, your suffering with the people of El Salvador . . . do you see?? These concerns extend far beyond personal safety and comfort. They are more than the fear of your personal death. They come out of the web of life in which you belong. What does that say? Does it say something about your power? What kind of power can we draw from this interconnectedness? Let's spend some time on that. I have some exercises that can help us explore what that power might be.*

Each guide has different words and images for this, distinctive experiences to draw from. Given my personal bent and professional focus, I tend to use spiritual metaphors. My colleague, Joseph Havens, uses ecological images, and speaks of the turning as a rediscovery of our interweaving roots and branches. My colleagues Sarah Pirtle and Molly Scott, who are musicians, invite participants to experience their turning as an opening into a shared world of rippling, intersecting vibrations. Philip Bennett, a philosophy professor, gives to his workshops new concepts, tells them of the hundredth monkey phenomenon and morphogenetic fields. And so can you, out of your own gifts and experiences, offer images and ways of thinking that are meaningful to you.

II
Methods for the Turning

Here are a variety of exercises that can be helpful to the group in making the connection or transition between despair and empowerment.

D/E Exercise 13

The Cradling

(30-60 Minutes)

In the last chapter I described a meditation on the body, which is conducted in pairs. I usually use it in the first part of a workshop because it is so effective in building the trust between participants that is essential to the sharing of deep feelings. Yet the Cradling is appropriate to any stage of the group process, because it enhances our awareness of the universality and interconnectedness of the life that has taken form in each of us. Most particularly it helps us make the key cognitive connection between power and open interrelatedness, that is evident in the evolution of living systems — and that is, in a sense, what the turning is all about.

D/E Exercise 17

Illustrated Mini-lecture on Power

(15 Minutes)

The connection between power and vulnerability is spelled out in a short "chalk-talk" I like to offer. It is the most standard means I personally employ for the turning. Here is an abbreviated version of it, with diagrams I sketch out on a large sheet of newsprint or chalkboard as I talk. It is based on the systems view set out in Chapter Two, as well as on the spiritual teachings mentioned there.

Let's look at our notions of what 'power' is. Those notions in any culture derive from that culture's worldview. In the dominant Western worldview over the last two millenia, reality has been seen as consisting of separate and discrete entities or substances. Atoms, molecules, plants, people, rocks . . . these separate entities, like so many billiard balls, are seen as what is **real**. *Whether you're classifying them like*

Aristotle or studying their motions like Newton, they make up the real world.

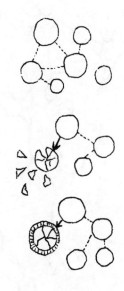

*What happens **between** these entities, that is their actions, communications, relationships, has been considered **less real,** because it cannot be seen or measured. It's hard to weigh or measure messages or energy exchanges, love or hate. Of course, in these interactions one entity can shove another around. That seems the most obvious measure of its power: power gets defined as domination. If the impact is forceful enough, one entity can damage or shatter another.*

If I am one of these entitles, then, I certainly want to protect myself, so I won't be wiped out; I want to ensure that I'll continue to exist. I build defenses — whether as a personality or as a nation-state. Defenses can take many forms: nuclear arms, numbness, belligerence, even the need to please. So, as you can see, power has become equated with invulnerability. To be powerful is to have strong defenses.

Let's note, too, that if power is seen in terms of the capacity to have your own way, to dominate others, it is a zero-sum game. The more someone else has, the less you have — and vice-versa. Power-over presupposes and creates a win-lose situation. You have got to win over if you are not to lose out.

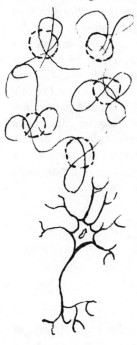

Now in our century the old view of reality, as being composed of separate, self-existent entities, has changed radically. Scientists have discovered that life phenomena are created and sustained by deep interconnections. They have turned the lens through which we can see the world, so that instead of beholding separate substances, we see flows and currents of energy, matter and information. Substances turn to process. What had appeared before as separate entities dissolve into flows, and are seen to be patterns in these flows — patterns that sustain each other by means of their relationships and exchanges. Atoms, cells, plants, people, societies . . . all are dynamic patterns, or open systems within systems. They influence each other so deeply that it is hard to decide where one leaves off and the other begins, indeed all boundaries are essentially arbitrary distinctions in this dynamic, flowing web.

A frequent image that systems scientists use, to convey the nature of this interconnectedness, is that of a nerve cell or neuron in a neural net.

That is how our brains and bodies work. It is also how

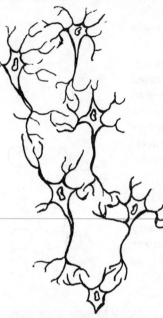

an ecosystem works, or a family or a society. We are each like a neuron within the neural net of an organ that in turn is a subsystem within a larger body.

Now what does this say about the nature of power? Of what does the power of a neuron consist? If power is equated with invulnerability, and I as a neuron build defenses around me, what happens to me? Yes, I become dysfunctional, I atrophy and weaken the larger system of which I am a part and on which I depend.

The power of a neuron lies in its capacity to open to the charge, open to the messages travelling through the larger body. From that capacity arise ever more intricate and appropriate responses. That is how we learn and how society learns; that is how intelligence flowers.

So now we see power in a new light. It is not invulnerability, but openness. It is not a zero-sum game (you win/I lose), but a win/win or lose/lose game. It is not power-over, but power-with — this is what systems scientists call **synergy**.

In a way we have known this all along. We know it because that is the direction of evolution: life forms as they evolve become ever more vulnerable to their environment, the better to connect and respond. And we know it because we experience synergy in our own lives. When we fall in love or raise a child or even play frisbee, we experience the personal sense of enhancement that comes from enhancing the potential of others. We also know it because our spiritual traditions attest to this kind of growth and potency. But having been conditioned by the old patriarchal paradigm of power, we are not accustomed to viewing and naming this capacity as **power**. It is important that we do so now, because our survival depends on our moving beyond the primitive, competitive, win/lose notions of power. And as we do, we can see how our very capacity to feel pain for the world can empower us to connect with it, and act to heal it.

D/E Method 18
Brainstorming
(15 Minutes)

In a brainstorm the group thinks together, like one collective brain. In and of itself, therefore, it is a good way to learn to appreciate our "neural" interconnectedness and synergy.

First, let's review the process of brainstorming itself, which has become increasingly popular over the last decade as a mode of collective problem-solving. Use a chalkboard or, preferably, large sheets of paper taped to the wall (these can be saved for later reference). Write the topic question of the brainstorm at the top, and invite a "scribe" to jot up the responses from the group. Everyone participates in this group-think and the faster the pace, the better. This is because some of our most original and insightful thoughts arise when we do not pause to analyze or censor them as odd or wild. One idea triggers another, and soon they are popping in rapid-fire succession. It is a great way to raise a group's energy, trust and spirits. For this to happen, remind the group of the three rules of brainstorming:

1. Say whatever occurs to you that is relevant to the question.

2. Don't explain or defend your ideas.

3. Don't judge or discuss the ideas of others.

The purpose is to generate ideas and approaches, not to evaluate them. Evaluation and analysis are types of mental activity which we can undertake later.

The brainstorms that I have found effective at *the Turning* are:

1. "In our daily lives what causes us to avoid expressing our deepest concerns and feelings about the dangers facing our world?" In Chapter One, I described such a brainstorm in a Baltimore workshop. It helps people to see how common yet how unnecessary are the considerations that cause us to repress our deepest responses to the threats of mass annihilation. Uncovering them together helps us to move beyond these obstacles, and enhance our sense of freedom and power.

2. "In what ways can we help others honor the deep concerns and feelings *they* may have about the dangers facing our world?" This question is very closely related to the first one, and often flows from it. It serves to reveal the power we have to help other people and the extent to which that power flows from our own capacity to experience inner pain.

Both exercises move us farther away from isolation and judgment, and toward a keener sense of our commonality and inherent copefulness.

D/E Exercise 19
Spontaneous Writing
(30-40 Minutes)

Choose a word, a theme or phrase. Put it up on the wall. Have everyone in the group relax, breathing deep and slow as they read it; and have them then take pen or pencil and write — spilling out, pouring out whatever comes to mind. Help them by your suggestions to release themselves from the judge and censor in their mind, and playfully or prayerfully to let come what comes. There is no requirement to read it to others.

"Out of this dark and painful stuff our task is to . . ." This half-sentence from Sister Carita is the catalyst I used for the spontaneous writing.

Coming after the evocation and sharing of our feelings of pain for the world (the first stage of the work), it lets the depths of the psyche speak its own knowings. It lets each person, still feeling the support of the group, move alone now and attentive into the inner chambers of the heart, there to listen to what only *that* heart can say. It lets each catch a fresh glimpse of his or her distinctive truth.

Out of this dark and painful stuff our task is to . . . experience it — to work with it as we have done here, to better know ourselves — to better love each other, loving strangers who are ourselves.   — Aerospace engineer

Out of this dark and painful stuff our task is to . . . see the points of light in the darkness, like gleams from scattered houses and farms you see at night from the plane window across the dark land. Each is a life, a hope. The task is to reach them, touch, speak, connect — grassroots organizing with groups like this — spinning fibres of light that intersect . . .
     — Insurance company executive

Through tears of sadness rainbows can be seen. Our pain is our own, yet it is also universal. It is in the net that connects us and it can set us free. It can set us free from isolation. Out of it comes the stuff that makes peace, and strength for the long days ahead, and compassion . . .
     — 17 year-old high school student

After ten or fifteen minutes of writing, people are almost invariably eager to share it. Let them do this in twos (with their buddy if you have used the buddy-system, as suggested in Chapter Four). Then, if there is time, the whole group can meet in a large circle, participants reading aloud passages that particularly struck them from what they or their partner wrote. In any case, let them tape the writings up on the wall, for the group to read at leisure. Each time I have used this exercise the group has spontaneously selected a member to collect, duplicate and mail them out to all participants.

Writer and peace advocate Gene Knudsen Hoffman taught me this method; sometimes she uses it in her workshops to generate poems. She says: "It was remarked to me 'Nobody can write a poem in ten minutes — it takes hours, sometimes months . . .' to which I responded: 'Nobody in my class writes anything in ten minutes. Each member has been preparing all his or her life to write whatever is written in a particular evening. Each of us is a new revelation with a portion of the truth to enlighten and guide each other.'"

D/E Exercise 20
The Well
(50-60 Minutes)

This experience is a form of collective listening and sharing out of silence — a form originally inspired by the Quaker form of worship. In it we let all our doings subside and simply face together the mystery of being alive in this planet-time, and we let that mystery speak to us out of inner stillness. In that reflective stillness it can speak to us deeply — through images from the past, through remembered faces and voices of other beings, through the reverberations of what was expressed in the despairwork, through spiritual teachings we have absorbed and which now find fresh utterance through us. Because the group interaction seems to come from our collective depths, we call this process *The Well*.

We sit in a circle, sometimes with a candle burning in the center. A guide offers the invitation to the listening, with words that help us be relaxed and attentive. For example:

Breathing deep, let us wait in stillness. Let us wait for what the world — the miracle of our being alive in it now — would have us know. Let that silence happen, as we attend to the images and thoughts that arise. After a while we may be moved to speak, or to share our listening through song or movement. Then we let speak that which wishes to be spoken through us. To let each sharing come out of the Well, let us allow a moment of silence between each one.

There is usually ten minutes or so of initial meditative quiet, often with eyes closed, before those that are gathered begin to speak, at random, one by one. Sometimes it is a story, sometimes a prayer, sometimes a song or a cry of pain. The gathered silence enwraps us and frees us from the moorings of our separate selfhood — and what then is spoken out of that silence speaks to us all and feeds us. In one *Well* experience, words were spoken that opened us to our grief for the children we knew and loved. Spontaneously, one by one, we began to say their names . . . Elissa, Sammy, George . . . letting them be present to us all, like a gift, and experiencing the depth of our caring. And a new song began to sing itself through our throats, a song that celebrated the ravaging, beautiful and indomitable power of our love for them.

In another Well, I remember, Humpty Dumpty was evoked. Humpty Dumpty, falling and breaking and all the king's men could not put him together agian — it felt good to give imaginal form to our sense of fragmentation. As we sat with that image, a voice among us slowly spoke, adding what she saw: from the shattered shell a bird rose into the air. Eggshells break to reveal new life; I had forgotten that. The very imagery that expressed our pain pointed to our hope.

At our Interhelp gathering on the New England coast we had a Well, too. A colleague from Colorado had picked up on the beach a net from a lobster trap, and it now was passed slowly from hand to hand. As each person fingered it, words were spoken, fresh images offered, for the strength we can find in each other through the powerful mystery of our interconnectedness. I have that piece of string net still, hung from a nail on the wall of my study. It reminds me of how we can feed each other spiritually, and how in that act we can "come home".

USING THE BODY

The Turning can also be experienced physically, in movement. It is through movement that we know we are alive. Movement can release depths of awareness that lie far below the level of words, and help us literally to *incorporate* what we have been discovering through the despairwork. It activates the innate knowledge of our interconnectedness. The next three exercises are offered by Sarah Pirtle, an Interhelp colleague and peaceworker in Western Massachusetts.

D/E Exercise 21
Embrace Tiger, Return to Mountain
(10 Minutes)

Here we draw from a sequence in Tai Chi, the Chinese movement meditation. To understand its import, let us recall the phenomenon of psychological projection.

As we saw in Chapter One, repressed material is often projected outwards onto other people or groups; these serve as targets or scapegoats for denied fears and angers and guilts about the condition of the world. One of the functions of despair-work is to help us own or retrieve our projections. Pirtle's Tai Chi exercise expresses this on a level that is both conscious and physical.

> *Visualize the "tiger" outside of yourself. It is the dark and painful part of your experience that you wish you could cast away. Slowly stepping forward, knees slightly bent, swing the arms wide and slow in an encompassing gesture to embrace the tiger. Slowly bring arms back toward the chest, taking the tiger with your breath into yourself — into the "whole" self. On the outbreath your arms swing back on either side, as the other leg steps even with the first to balance your weight. You are now "returned to mountain," in a dynamic state of rest. Repeat and explore the movements, slowly, attentively. Try to see the tiger more clearly each time; engage in silent dialogue with whatever tiger becomes vivid for you. Each time, as you take it in, feel the massiveness of the mountain to which you return. Grounded there, sense your poise — rock-steady, open, and sure.*

D/E Exercise 22
Twin-Hand Movements
(10 Minutes)

Group participants enter into movement dialogue with each other. People pair up and rest the back of their right hand against the back of their partner's right hand. They take turns leading arm movements, wide gestures in, out, up, down, around, this way and that — ever maintaining contact through the back of the hands. When it is their turn to follow, they need to have their feet firmly planted *and* to stay flexible enough to remain connected with the changing movements. The challenge is not a difficult one, but it reveals something about the kind of power that is intrinsic to open systems. As we saw in Chapter Two, evolution moves toward ever increased sensitivity and flexibility. Those capacities allow responsive interplay, and we attend to them in this exercise.

This exercise is also very useful at the outset of a workshop to help people "open out/tune in."

D/E Exercise 23
Opening Pathways through Movement
(15 Minutes)

Have music playing. (Pirtle uses instrumental music at the beginning, such as the Paul Winter Consort, Do'a, Kay Gardiner. Toward the end, she uses song with lyrics, such as "Lay Down Your Burden" from Paul Winter's Common Ground or Joan Baez's "Open the Door and Come On In.")

Let each person find a space in the room big enough to make large gestures without bumping into others. Most participants prefer to work with their eyes closed: it helps them center and sense their own inner dynamics.

Here is how Pirtle guides this exercise, with initial instructions and through successive stages of "waking," "reaching," and "connecting."

- *Trust what your body says. Find the movements you want to do. If a movement feels stuck or boring, change it. Try something new.*

- *We want to open up all the cells of the body so that we can feel the energy and love passing through us. Let's start with our hands and give attention to each finger. Begin with one finger and do what you need to do. Gently stretch that finger, move it in circles. You will know when you are ready to move on to the next part of your hand. Consciously awaken your whole hand: all of your fingers, your palm, your wrist. Spend as long as each part needs. (In this section you can either guide the group through different body parts or invite them to go through their whole body at their own pace.) Feel the flow of energy inside your body. Imagine that the music is carrying light and color inside you. Let the music wash inside you, bathe you, move you. Imagine the way your body opens to the music to let it in. Does it flow with your breath? Does it come in through your heart? your palms?*

- *We have wonderful long appendages for reaching out into the world. We are resilient living parts of the web. Keep your clear focus inside and at the same time reach out and feel your connections. Reach out with all five points of your star — both arms, both legs, head. Explore gently and curiously into the space around you. Reach high and low into areas you might have neglected. Feeling quick and silly we can jab and stab in many directions.*

- *Continue reaching, continue listening to your own body and how you want to move. Opening your eyes, if they are closed, become aware of all the others in this room with you. Moving at your own pace, begin to move around the web, reaching out and contacting. Reach with hands, elbows, heads, knees, feet — aware that you are part of this larger living organism.*

You may want to move slow or quick, oozing like honey or zipping like a waterbug. Now stop. Freeze. Look around and breathe. Reach out to the nearest person to massage a hand or shoulder.

The exercise reaches completion as people connect and small groups form for a following activity of discussion and planning.

D/E Exercise 24
The Dance for Life
(2 Hours)

Annie Prutzman, another facilitator and one who is acquainted with Native American spiritual traditions, has developed a ritual that she calls the *Dance for Life*. I had the good fortune to participate in it one fall day in Northern California. I will describe it very briefly in terms of its four parts; and as I do, please note: (a) the retrieval of psychological projections, and (b) the passage through darkness to light, or through pain to power, which is characteristic of the turning.

1. **Introduction, warm-up, invocation, and purification.** Annie explained the ancient uses of ritual and dance: to help people tune to the world of nature, the needs of society, and our own inner voices. Those old ways still live in our memory as a species, still are available to us if we harken to them. She explained the procedures we would follow throughout the entire ritual. Some bodywork and breathing exercises helped us relax, warm up. The ritual itself then began, as Annie invoked the presence of other beings and natural forces in the web of life, helping us to be more aware of the cosmic setting in which we exist. She passed an abalone shell with burning sage to purify the room and each of us in it.

2. **The Demon Dance.** Given a crayon and paper, each of us was instructed to find our "spot" in the room, one that felt good to us. Each of us then — and this took some inner listening — drew, with our nondominant hand, a picture or symbol of the demon we would address. Like Sarah's Tiger, this demon represents some part of our world that we hate or fear, or some aspect of ourself that we would reject. As the drumbeat began, we let that demon dance through us, move through our bodies, sound through our larynx — in grunts, shouts, songs. The energy and movement in the room mounted to a violent pitch, peaked and then slowly subsided. At that point we found ourselves in a circle, and one by one each went to the flame that was lit in the center, and burned the image of his or her demon. (No talking throughout)

3. **Dance for Life.** Returning to our "spots" in the room, we began to dance alone, expressing how we felt after releasing the demon. Slowly to the drumbeat, we began to move around the room,, began to dance in relation to others, letting our movements interact in pairs and then other pairs, till the whole circle found itself spontaneously moving in concert.

4. **Circle of Hope.** Quiet now, we sat in a circle, reflecting. Annie passed out candles and lit one from the central flame. Slowly one by one each person lit their candle from the next. As we did, we spoke aloud our hopes and intentions for our common world. When all the candles were alight, the ritual began to draw to a close with spontaneous chanting, songs, and prayers. It was a long closing, for no one wanted to leave.

D/E Exercise 25
The Web: A Guided Meditation
(15-20 Minutes)

This spoken meditation arose at the turning point of a workshop offered in Washington, D.C. in the first year of the work. It is most effective if participants can stretch out.

Lie, stretch . . . relax into floor, letting go . . .

Feel breath . . . lungs, abdomen . . . glide on the breath . . . in, out . . . . Feel how this breathing is happening, how it is not something you are deciding to do, making yourself do . . . rather it is happening to you, you are being breathed, life is breathing you . . . . As it breathes everyone in this room, everyone in this world . . . in and out . . . as life is breathing an African child, a Russian soldier, President _____ . . . at this very moment, as if we were one . . . . As you feel your breath feel these interconnections . . .

The oxygen ignites each cell . . . stirs it awake as it burns in the metabolism of life . . . . extend your consciousness deep within to feel this energy . . . . This energy streams out of your body, too . . . from your head, from your fingers, from your toes . . . . Extend your consciousness out along these filaments of energy . . . . Picture them, like threads of light perhaps, gossamer-thin, pulsing . . . . They interconnect and interweave with the energies of everyone else in this room . . . like a web which sustains you.

The web extends beyond this room, for it is made of relationships. . . woven of the flows and interconnections that interlace you with this universe . . . . Experience now the great multiplicity of strands. . . .

Relationships formed by the love and work and laughter and tears you've shared with other beings . . . . They extend across space, across time . . . . They shape what you are . . . . They sustain and give you place . . . . Sense those filaments, lie into them . . .

The web sustaining you is made of stuff too . . . your bones and muscles, blood and skin, concocted so intricately out of the food you've eaten . . . out of grains and vegetables and fruit and meat . . . grown in so many and far-off places . . . . The grass and the munching jaws of the cow as she makes her milk, for butter, cheese for you . . . . The soil that held and fed and yielded the grain for your bread, the boughs of the tree that bore the orange for your juice . . . . The hands that plowed and sowed and reaped . . . and processed . . . . All these processes feed into you and you are them . . .

Back through time this web extends . . . mothers and fathers, our great-grandmothers and great-grandfathers . . . giving us our coloring and features, our tricks of wit . . . . We can see them in our gestures . . . hear them in our voice . . . . The web extends back through countless genera-tions. . . through the numberless ancestors we share . . . all the way back to our brothers and sisters with gills and wings . . . for it is of star stuff evolv-ing that we all are made in the flowing of time . . . we are called into being out of these flows, sustained by them . . . rest in them now . . . . We are each a jewel in this vast net, where intelligence and compassion can ignite at each node . . . . Sounds of a gull wisping across the surface of the ocean . . . sights of mountains rising out of the earth . . . colors of the sunrise. . . scents of pine . . . the excitement of a new idea . . . the melody of a favorite song . . .

There is pain, too, that comes in along the strands of the web . . . a close friend in distress . . . reports of an oil spill . . . a Lebanese mother weeping for her lost children . . . do not shut them out, they inhere in the web of this space-time . . . open to these sorrows, breathe them in, so the channels may stay open for the flow of energy and life and change . . . . If we block the pain, we block the joy out too . . . . There is energy in the flow-ing of this fluid net, love that has enriched us, love that we give . . . . Feel the caring and love that flow out from you, through you . . .

Open to the pulsing of the web, its murmurs, whispers, tugs . . . it is through that vast network that forms were shaped and intelligence arose and love . . . all of it: the tears and laughter shaped you, as it shaped the mockingbird and the deep diving trout . . . you are of it. . . of it, even to the terror that we have unleashed now . . . open to it all, unafraid, relaxed, alert . . . . We are the universe knowing itself . . . like cells in the mind of God . . .

To all our brothers and sisters we open now . . . in this dark time . . . . We go now through a dark place, but we do not go alone . . . . And we do not go without our own timeless knowledge of the dark . . . . We come from it, it is behind our eyes . . . . And we will look into it until the dark itself is clear . . .

and home . . . and we draw strength from it . . . sustained in the vastness of the web . . . known, cradled . . .

Still sensing these connections we stretch now, open our eyes, slowly move to rise . . .

Chapter Seven

Stage Three:
Empowerment Work

We have only begun to know
the power that lies in us if we would join
our solitudes in the communion of struggle.

So much is unfolding that must
complete its gesture,

so much is in bud.   **—Denise Levertov, from** *Beginners*

Ralph Nader, who has motivated thousands to work for social change, was asked in an interview in 1982 what he considered to be **the** most important issue facing us right now and for the rest of the decade. "It is," he said, "how to overcome the widespread feeling among people that they don't count in terms of affecting the use of power in the world. That has often been called citizen apathy; but it is a function of powerlessness. And nothing proceeds to remedy victimization in this world of ours until. . .they feel self-confidence that they can find out about issues and act on them."

As we saw in Chapter One, this pervasive sense of powerlessness derives to a substantial degree from feelings of hopelessness in the face of threats of mass annihilation, and most particularly from the repression of these feelings. Every act of denial and avoidance is an admission of futility that is self-fulfilling. As we have stressed in this book the very process of unblocking our pain for the world releases energy, clarifies thought, breaks down isolation. Not only is despairwork itself empowering in these ways, it also can help us to free ourselves from old linear notions of power as domination and to redefine the mutual nature of our power as open systems.

We are now ready to describe the last section of the workshops. At this point we offer methods for recognizing the power in our lives and for using it to become effective agents for social change. The following workshop activities can be drawn upon and adapted to enable participants:

1. To experience the power within us, recognizing our own adequacy and our capacity to choose.

2. To broaden our vision of what is possible, and to see it clearly enough that our resolve and will are strengthened.

3. To acquire skills for social change work.

I

Experiencing the Power Within Us

In the mini-lecture in the previous chapter, we redefined power and saw its relation to our capacity to feel pain for the world. In this kind of power we do not rely on ourselves alone, but on the web in which we take being, whether we define this web in systems terms or in spiritual terms. The following methods help us to recognize it at work in our lives.

D/E Exercise 26
How We Experience Our Power
(15-20 Minutes)

Think of a time, or times in your life when you felt powerful. When something important and good happened because of a choice you made, because of something you said or did, because of the way you were. Choose one of these times . . . recapture the scene . . . play it back for yourself. . . . What made you feel powerful in this situation? Now in groups of four tell that story, taking turns and listening to each other without comment until you all have finished.

People are not accustomed to sharing this kind of experience, yet it is important to do so. It helps us to recognize our capacity to create positive change. At this point of the workshop, an incident often comes to mind that a participant would not previously have labeled an exercise of power. "I found myself simply talking to the guard at the gate of the nuclear power plant . . ." "I was presiding at the board of directors' meeting, and I felt stuck; I decided to relinquish my accustomed role as leader, and then suddenly everyone was able to decide what to do." Many say that it had not occurred to them before that their flexibility, and ability to make others effective, could be a form of power.

The potency of this exercise struck me most forcibly when I saw my husband Francis lead it. Together we were guiding a despair and empowerment weekend at Pendle Hill, the Quaker study center. Fran, who is trained in gestalt therapy, was facilitating the exercise in a circle of participants. One man, Jim, said that he experienced no power in his life. "What gives you pleasure?" Fran asked. "Well . . . I don't know . . . . I feel good when I ride my bicycle." "What is that like?" asked Fran. "Well, I tell you now, it feels good when I'm riding home from work and the traffic is jammed. I just speed by all those stuck cars and trucks, they can hardly move and I'm going where I want to go." "That sounds like a powerful feeling," says Fran. "You bet!" said Jim beaming, . . ."I guess that *is* a kind of power, isn't it?" And he recognized with pride the guerilla-power of ingenuity and flexibility which (as I noted to myself on the sidelines) is exactly the kind of power evidenced in nature, in the successful adaptibility of open systems.

D/E Exercise 27
How We Image Our Power
(30 Minutes)

Our sense of the power that is in us can be hard to convey in words. Close your eyes and breathe deep and become aware of what your power is like . . . . Let images or sensations or sounds emerge for you. Now take the paper and colors and begin to draw how your power appears to you at this moment.

After five minutes or so, the drawings are shared in small groups. They show inner capacities (a heart with a sun in it), or outer dimensions (a tree with deep roots and many creatures rooting in its branches). One woman drew a river winding through the landscape, and in its curly rushing waters were many objects: first nuclear missiles and cooling towers, stick figures of soldiers and hungry children, and then as the river progressed, trees, flowers, birds, musical notes. "My power is not to close myself off any more, but to be open to the horror and awfulness, to let it all flow through me, and to let it change into what I choose to make happen. These tributaries flowing in, are all the people who are doing the same thing. So I guess it isn't *my* river or *my* power anymore, but everybody's."

The drawing of one man, an engineer, appeared to be a huge fish net. "I started to draw my anger, see this part here is a gun, but then it started connecting with the anger of others, and then with their needs, and then with their hopes. And now I'm not sure which part of the net I am. I am part of it all. I guess that is my power."

"I drew a dream I had the other night," said a university professor. As we looked we debated whether it was a tree or a mushroom cloud or a human brain, for her drawing had the shape of each. "Don't ask me," she said. Then we decided it was all three: that it showed how our intelligence and choice can change the mushroom cloud into the tree of life, and in that choice is our power.

D/E Exercise 28
How Others Empower Us
(30-40 Minutes)

T.H. White in the *Sword and the Stone*, tells us the story of King Arthur as a boy. I have recounted this in workshops because it portrays the dimensions of power available to us as open interconnected systems.

The wizard Merlin, as Arthur's tutor, schooled the boy in wisdom by turning him into various creatures and had him live, for brief periods, as a falcon, an ant, a wild goose, a badger, a carp in the palace moat . . . . The time came when the new King of All England was to be chosen; it would be he who could draw the sword from the stone. All the famous knights, who came to the great tournament, went to the churchyard where the stone mysteriously stood, and tried mightily to yank out the sword that was imbedded in it. Heaving and sweating, they competed to prove their superior strength. No deal; tug and curse as they might, the sword did not budge. When the disgruntled knights departed to return to their jousting, Arthur, who was just a teenager then, lingered behind, went up to the stone to try his own luck. Grasping the sword's handle he pulled with all his strength, until he was exhausted and drenched. The sword remained immobile. Glancing around, he saw in the shrubbery surrounding the churchyard the forms of those with whom he had lived and learned. There they were: badger, falcon, ant and the others. As he greeted them with his eyes, he opened again to the powers he had known in each of them — the industry, the cunning, the quick boldness, the perseverance . . . knowing they were with him, he turned back to the stone and, breathing easy, drew forth from it the sword, as smooth as a knife from butter.

After hearing the story we learn through the following exercise how we, like the boy Arthur, can find our powers enhanced by others.

*You have a task before you. It has to do with creating a peaceful world. This task often seems impossible to accomplish. It is as difficult as pulling a sword from a boulder. Let this task, for the moment, **become** the removal of the sword. Feel the grain of the stone — how rough and unyielding it is,* *how rock-solid the sword is anchored in it right up to the hilt. Feel how it can't be moved by your individual desperate attempts, no matter how hard you strain and pull. You are now straining and pulling at it, your body tense, jerking with the effort . . . . The sword does not budge. Now look about your life, as Arthur looked about in the churchyard. See around the edges appearing from behind the bushes and shrubs the beings who have been important in your life. Some you may live and work with now, some may have lived a long time ago. But their vision, their qualities don't die; they live still. Let these beings appear: loved ones, teachers, saints, leaders, animals, even precious objects that have been teachers to you. Breathe in the joy and recognition you feel in beholding each of them. Think of the qualities in each you love and admire . . . breathe them in . . . . These qualities are already in you or else you would not be able to recognize them. Feel their energy quickening in you, these friends are smiling at you, reminding you of what you have in common and what is available to you now. The courage, the intellect, the goodness, and power that poured through their lives can also be yours. Feel their energy and insight pour through from the one web in which we all take being. Breathing in these strengths, reach for the handle of the sword, slowly, easily — now draw it out. See how the sword answers not to your own separate ego-efforts, but to the power of all beings, as you open to them.*

After the story and the guided fantasy participants in the group can share with each other the sources from which they draw power.

Who appears in the surrounding bushes of your life and gives you strength to pull the sword from the stone? Who gives you insight and courage? It could be a grandfather or a third grade teacher, Mahatma Gandhi, or Martin Luther King . . . . The gifts they received from the web of life are available to you as well.

At this point of the workshop I offer the guided meditation on the *Great Ball of Merit*, which is in Chapter Eight. Given time constraints, I usually offer it in lieu of the boy Arthur story. It helps us to expand our awareness of the sources available to us, and to realize that we're not alone in the effort to save our world, nor can we do so by our own individual efforts. The gifts of others in the "neural net" provide us momentum and support.

II

Clarifying Our Vision

We need now to see, as clearly as we can, how and for what purposes we can use the power that we draw from many sources. Choices are available to us at each point of our lives, but these choices can appear trivial, unless we have a clear vision of the future. Our dreaming muscles may be atrophied, but we can exercise and develop them. For the future is not out there in front of us, but inside us. Like the moth in the caterpillar's cocoon, it is hidden in us and that is why it cannot be seen. If you poke open the cocoon prematurely all you see is an undifferentiated glue. But the structure of the new creature is there already present in what scientists call the "imaginal cells." When the time is come, these cells constellate, take form.

A number of activities can serve to clarify this future that we can let take shape in us. Here are some that tap the powers of our imagination. Each helps to break the stranglehold of the immediate present and lets us step beyond it to envisage what we could bring to be.

D/E Exercise 29
Fantasy on Choosing Your Life
(15-20 Minutes)

This guided fantasy was invented by Dr. Carol Wolman, though she might prefer to say that it "came through" her. Carol is the psychiatrist who first studied and publicized the psychological effects of nuclear weapons; as such she is a founding mother of despair and empowerment work. I was there at a meeting on a California farm where she first, spontaneously, led this exercise. Since then I have shared it in many workshops, like a gift she gave me to pass on; it is one of my favorite group exercises.

Close your eyes and imagine that, sometime before your birth, you are wandering through the universe. You hear that a small planet in a distant solar system is approaching its evolutionary crisis: the dominant intelligent species is creating weapons of total annihilation and will be forced to choose between extinction and a quantum leap in consciousness. Perhaps you have been through it before, perhaps you have a debt to pay; you decide to take a human body on Earth to help out in this critical time. So, out in the halls of space, perhaps on the planet Uranus, you meet with the Incarnation Committee. You discuss with its members the part you want to play in the drama unfolding on Earth, you clarify the particular work you will do. The Committee presents you with a series of decisions to make. Remember them now: you are gifted with total recall and can remember the choices you made that brought you into this present life.

- *Choose a date of birth — a year to be born relative to 1945, the year of the bombing of Hiroshima and Nagasaki. You decide whether to be born before or after this event, and how near to it in Earthyears, for that timing will affect the perspective you bring. You also select, in the Earth's orbit around the sun, a point for your birth which determines the season and the planetary array, and you may decide to give yourself clues in your horoscope that will help you remember, later on, what you are supposed to be doing.*

• *Choose a spot on Earth — a climatic zone, a country, a region. You weigh the decision whether to incarnate in the United States, and work from "the belly of the beast."*

• *You choose an ethnic and racial form that will best enable you to express yourself, and a social-economic class that will provide you with the challenges or benefits you will need to prepare for your work.*

• *You select a spiritual tradition into which to be born, that will provide some of the thoughtforms and rituals that can help you, or you may choose not to receive a religious upbringing at all.*

• *Choose a gender. What sex will provide for you the particular opportunities and challenges you will need?*

• *Now, most important of all, you choose your parents. You pick a mother and father, knowing that they have strengths and qualities that you can draw on, and that the difficulties you experience with them will help prepare you for the work you are to do.*

• *Similarly you choose whether you will have siblings, and your relation to them in age. They may be souls you have known before. Your choice is made with the knowledge that the loneliness, companionship and conflict in your family will provide you important lessons for your mission on planet Earth.*

• *Lastly, you choose a name. It may be the name given you by your parents, or it may be a secret name, to be discovered within yourself as you find your distinctive role.*

• *Once you have made all those decisions, you are born as a human infant and forget all that went before. But those choices were effective, for here you are now! Though it seems sometimes that the circumstances of your birth and life are imposed by external forces, you gradually rediscover why you are here — and how wisely you chose. For every factor in your life can assist you now in the important work you have come to do.*

FANTASIES ABOUT TALKING WITH A CHILD IN THE FUTURE

*Formerly the future was simply given to us; now it must be achieved
We must become the agriculturists of time. If we do not plant and
cultivate the future years of human life, we will never reap them . . . .
The nuclear peril makes all of us, whether we happen to have
children of our own or not, the parents of all future generations.*
— Jonathan Schell, *The Fate of the Earth*

The following three exercises of the imagination touch the core of our resolve to ensure a future for humanity. They challenge us to re-establish our ties to the future — ties that have been broken by our anticipation of nuclear holocaust. We can do this now, at any point, by engaging in imaginative dialogue with a child in the future. Here are three different paths that can lead us into such dialogue, as they have been developed respectively by Barbara Hazard, by Charles Varon and Kevin McVeigh, and by myself. Perhaps after engaging in them, you will find yourself creating your own distinctive version.

D/E Exercise 30
Imagining a World Without Threat
(40 Minutes)

Because participants will be asked to draw after the visualization they should have paper and crayons close to them.

Get comfortable, relax, close your eyes.

*Let come to mind images of some of the young people you know . . .
maybe even some who are not born yet who will be close to you . . . .
Choose one whom you feel close to . . . . Take a walk together . . . go to a
favorite place, one special to you . . . . Find a comfortable spot . . . sit
with the child . . . . Notice how it looks and feels: weather . . . sunny or
gray? warm or cool? time of day . . . of year? Smells? Sounds?*

*Turn to the child and talk to him or her . . . . Now tell him or her that
the danger is over — the danger of nuclear war, of disasters to the planet, of
pollution. Explain what that means to his or her life, to yours and others',
and to the earth . . . . You will have two minutes to talk to the child; it will
be plenty of time . . . .*

*Now touch the child in whatever way is appropriate and let him or her
leave. Know that she or he will be all right . . . . Allow yourself to feel how
it was to do that, to know that the danger is over, to be in that place and to
love the child and the world deeply. Notice what images arise . . . . maybe
a scene, people, animals, places . . . maybe simply colors, lines and shapes . . .*

maybe no images . . . this is true of many people, it's no problem . . . don't worry . . . . Notice if there's a feeling of movement in your body, your hands . . . a gesture . . . . Allow the images to come freely and notice if one seems stronger . . . . You'll have two minutes to do this . . . .

Now bringing your images, colors, shapes of gestures back with you, feel the paper in front of you. Let your hand move over it with your eyes closed. When you're ready, open your eyes and choose a color or colors . . . begin to draw whatever came to you. You may want to keep your eyes closed if that's more comfortable for you, or draw with your non-dominant hand. You'll have all the time you need to do this.

When the participants finish drawing, they turn over the paper and begin writing on the back. They write whatever comes to mind, non-stop, to the bottom of the sheet. They are told that there is no need for it to "make sense" nor for them to show it to others later. Afterwards, however, most of them are eager to share what came to them — and they are given the opportunity to do so in the large group or in small groups, depending on the time available and the number of participants. They will enjoy putting them up on the wall, for the sharing of this work is important.

Here is a poem that was written during this exercise:

> *The promise of peace*
> *Forbidden, long hoped for,*
> *Goes on like the hills*
> > *in an infinite dream.*
> *Go forth you young warriors*
> *To conquer your thought-forms*
> *Transforming them*
> *Mightily from dragons*
> > *to tears to hands holding*
> *Eyes meeting . . . .*
> > *Knowing the future*
> *Was meant for great ventures.*
> > — Phyllis Levin, Redway, CA

D/E Exercise 31
Envisioning Our Descendants
(20-30 Minutes)

Find a place to lie down and be comfortable . . . . Close your eyes and let your breathing become slower and deeper. Notice any places of tension in your body and breathe right into those places, allowing them to let go and relax.

Now, think for a moment of your youngest living descendant. It may be your child, or a nephew or niece, or a baby yet to be born . . . . Imagine that some time has passed and this person has had a child of his or her own. Picture this new baby. Does it look like you at all? . . .

Now allow this baby to grow up, to become an adult. Picture the baby he or she brings into the world. Notice the eyes, the chin, the color of hair . . . . This descendant grows up and, in time, becomes ready to have a child, too. The thread of life continues, and another generation, a new baby, is born.

We're about a century in the future. See this child taking its first steps; watch it mature from infancy to early childhood. Notice physical features — hair color, complexion, eyes, hands, shape of body . . . . Perhaps this child lives in a world that is free of the imminent threat of nuclear war. What does the child say to you? Perhaps the child thanks you for the work you did in your lifetime to ensure the world's continuance. Listen to the child for a few minutes . . . .

What do you tell your descendant about what it was like for you facing the nuclear threat in the 20th century? . . .

Now for the next few moments, let yourself be with this child. Perhaps the two of you continue to talk; perhaps you are together in silence.

Now, gradually take leave of the child. Consider for a moment that this may be the beginning of a new relationship — a personal relationship with someone yet to be born, and that such a relationship can be nourished and developed. It can become a source of strength and wisdom, giving a larger context to your life.

Know that you can return again to this future any time you want — that you can be with this child, this child living deep in nuclear time. And now, feel yourself returning slowly to the present, to 1983. When you are ready, open your eyes.

D/E Exercise 32
Thirty Years Hence
(15 Minutes)

As you guide this exercise, help participants to relax, as suggested above.

Put yourself forward in time. It is a day just like this, but thirty years from now. The year on the calendar has a different number, but you are still you, same name, same gestures and feelings and skin, same action of heart and lungs. Some of us may be pretty ancient by then, but let's assume you are still around and in one of your favorite spots. Don't worry about figuring out how the world has changed, just know that there is one key difference. And that is: all weapons have been dismantled, the world is disarmed. It may have happened back in the late eighties or early nineties; by now you have become so accustomed to the idea, you take it for granted.

*Now a child approaches you, about 8 or 9 years old. She has heard, perhaps from the songs and stories about those times, what you and your co-workers did back then to save the world from disaster. She approaches timidly, but with great curiosity. "Were there **really** bombs that could blow up the whole world?" Listen to her questions and hear how you answer them. "Where there **really** millions and millions of people who were sick and hungry?" . . . "What was it like to be alive in a time like that? Weren't you frightened?" . . . And lastly she asks, "What did you do to get through that scary time, and not be discouraged? . . . . What helped you stay strong, so you could know what to do?" . . . . And listen now to your answers.*

D/E Exercise 33
Imagining a World Without Weapons
(1-2 Hours)

This is the name of the workshops designed by Elise Boulding and Warren Ziegler to develop our capacity to invent and envisage alternative futures. The group process draws on our analytical as well as intuitive skills and enhances our belief that we *can* walk away from the brink of disaster and create together a liveable world. A number of us have incorporated elements of this process into despair and empowerment work; here is a sequence used by Sarah Pirtle. Before beginning the process she offers music (with songsheets) to inspire images (e.g. "Vine and Fig Tree," and "Last Night I Had the Strangest Dream.")

1. **Enter a world without weapons.** Pick a date, say thirty years from the day, and ask the group to imagine that we are not gathered to prevent nuclear war, but to celebrate the fact that there is no longer a danger of nuclear war. "Let that in. How does your body feel? Is your breathing different? Your shoulders less tense? What are your plans now for the coming year?" By these and other questions the group is guided to enter this imagined future.

2. **Write headlines in Small Groups.** Groups of six are provided with newsprint and markers. Closing our eyes we move deeper into the chosen year. (e.g. "Where are you standing? What do you hear, touch, smell? Who do you see around you and what are they doing? What are the forms of transportation? the international agreements? . . . . ") It is important that we place ourselves *inside* this new time rather than viewing it from afar. After this silent period, the groups open their eyes, select a scribe, and begin to share images. Then we choose a type of newspaper appropriate to the kinds of images that emerged and proceed to create headlines. In the process we are often surprised by our own inventiveness; a positive future becomes more concrete and believable. When finished, each set of headlines is presented to the whole gathering.

3. **Fill in the Intervening History.** Moving backwards from the chosen date toward the present, we reflect on what needs to have happened for these developments to occur. A scribe can jot these events on a time-line; the key thing is that we are looking from a weaponless future backwards, rather than from our usual vantage point on *this* side of our present obstacles. We then are invited to think of work that is being done right now that fits into this backwards history, and to share good news from the present.

4. **Reflecting on Our Resistance.** To live toward a positive future we need to acknowledge what holds us back from working to create it. The group can brainstorm the question, "What fears do we have about being successful in stopping nuclear war?"

5. **Closing.** Before ending with some songs expressing hope and determination, we can share what we have learned by going through this process and offer new images that have emerged, (e.g. One participant said she felt like an amphibian in the process of evolving.)

D/E Exercise 34
Collages of a Peaceful World
(60 Minutes)

Artwork, of course, provides an excellent avenue for reaching our incipient dreams for the future. One method is to engage participants in constructing collages with posterboard, magazines, crayons, bits of cloth and other materials. "What would a world of peace and justice look like?" There is no speaking. Cutting and pasting, handling the textures, colors, help make this a time of relaxed reflection. World Peacemakers who use this in their workshops say, "We have found this experience allows people to find in themselves a vision for the future they didn't know they had."

III
Developing Skills and Strategies

Now we can work together to develop some skills we need to realize our visions of the future. These skills involve: setting achievable goals, assessing our resources, planning actions, communicating our purposes, and enlisting the cooperation of others.

When we undertake the following activities in the context of a workshop, we are not usually planning a specific action or even pursuing specific goals as a group. Indeed the group may not meet again. We are enhancing our competencies as agents for social change.

D/E Exercise 35

Identifying Goals and Resources

(45 Minutes)

Participants work in pairs, taking turns. In response to questions from the facilitator, one speaks while the other records his or her answers with pen and paper; they then reverse roles. The questions from the guide run like this:

1. *If you were totally fearless and in the possession of all your powers, what would you do to heal our world?*

2. *What strengths or resources do you now have, that would help you do that?*

3. *What will you need to learn or acquire?*

4. *What obstacles are you likely to put in the way of fulfilling this goal?*

5. *What can you do in the next 24 hours — no matter how small the step — that will help you reach that goal?*

When each partner has recorded the other's answers, they take turns reading them back to each other. It can be potent to hear your intentions and resources uttered in another's voice; it helps you to appreciate them and take them seriously. The papers are then exchanged, so that you can take your own answers home as a reminder.

D/E Exercise 36
Planning Actions
(1 - 2 Hours)

This three-part exercise is adapted from processes developed by the Movement for a New Society; I have offered it in South Asian villages and American campuses, and found it equally powerful — and empowering — in both settings. It dramatizes how a group can think and work together, and how it can move from a general or abstract goal to immediate, specific and concrete actions.

1. **Envisioning Goals.** (45 Minutes) From categories listed on a board or paper, participants are invited to select which aspect of a desired future they wish to envision: education, health, food production and processing, communications, transportation? They are encouraged to choose an area in which they lack expertise, for it is the amateurs who often bring the most novel and ingenious ideas. They then convene in simultaneous topic-specific groups.

   First, in silence, each person dreams a bit and then jots on paper notions of an ideal way that that particular aspect of society might work (5 Minutes). Then they take turns sharing their ideas with their group, while a scribe in each records them on newsprint. The group then chooses the 4 or 5 ideas it finds most appealing (15 Minutes). The different groups then report these ideas to the whole gathering (15 Minutes).

   Note: If time is short, this part of the exercise can be omitted.

2. **Progressive Brainstorm.** (20 Minutes) Having heard these ideas, the whole group chooses one it wishes to focus on. Note: the specific issue *per se* is less important than the experience of bringing our collective creativity to bear on it. (If we have skipped the first stage of small group visioning, we can pick a goal at random, say clean air or free public transportation.) Writing the goal at the top of a sheet of paper, the group begins to brainstorm: what conditions would this goal necessitate? (See rules for brainstorming in Chapter Six).

   Take the goal of clean air. What conditions would free us from air pollution? These are listed in stage one of the brainstorm. Then the group chooses one of these ideas, say reduce the use of automobiles. That is written at the top of another sheet of paper and the group moves quickly onto a second brainstorm: What would we need to do to reduce the use of automobiles? Many ideas surface there, too; (mandatory carpools, blocked streets, public bicycles, new forms of mass transit). Again one of these is chosen, and on another sheet of paper it is brainstormed further as to how it might be implemented. The process is repeated and each time the ideas that are generated become more and more specific. Each lap of the brainstorm should not take more than four or five minutes. The process continues until actions are suggested that are so concrete, say, in this case, a door-to-door canvas to enlist support for a cooperative bicycle delivery system, that each person could conceivably do something about it in the next 24 hours. From the distant goal of clean air the group-think has moved to specific and immediate steps. At this point the group moves into the third component of the exercise.

3.   **Role-play.** Now that we have an immediate (though still hypothetical) action to undertake, how will we obtain the resources and cooperation we need? How will we enlist people? What persons or types of persons present a particular challenge? It is highly useful here to role-play such encounters, for it is at this juncture that we often feel blocked and some of our finest ideas remain just that — ideas.

Take the above example: We have decided to organize a cooperative delivery system by bicycle, and for that purpose teams will call on everyone in the community to elicit their support and involvement. We role play conversations between team members and senior citizens or high school students or the owner of a bicycle store or an official in the Highway Department.

The exercise is as instructive as it is entertaining. It forces us to discover how well we can think on our feet, what we need to know and say in order to be convincing. By reversing roles in mid-conversation, it gives us insight into the thoughts and feelings of the persons we are trying to convince. It breaks us out of polarized we-them thinking, and in letting us identify with others, it enhances our confidence and effectiveness.

D/E Exercise 37
Communicating Information
(30-40 Minutes)

Many of us are reluctant to speak our views about the condition of the world, because we feel we don't know enough facts to be convincing. It is hard to remember all the information that we have absorbed and that has motivated us to take action. Called upon to document the causes of our distress for the world, or the reasons why we protest the current state of affairs, we feel often tongue-tied, stupid, frustrated.

How do we block ourselves? And how can we move beyond these internal obstacles?

Kevin McVeigh offers an exercise that helps us to answer these questions, and to become more effective communicators. In doing so he reminds us that (1) We often have beliefs about our ability to recall facts that stem from our school experience, and that we need to identify and move beyond these beliefs. (2) We actually remember a great deal more than we think we do. His exercise demonstrates this.

We may begin by asking who, in the group, has difficulty in conveying information about the nuclear threat, who gets caught in a conversation and suddenly feels at a loss, forgetting what they thought they knew. A volunteer stands up in front of the group, "What do you know about the nuclear threat?" we ask. This may stymie them. "I feel stupid. See, I can't remember anything." "How does that feel?" The volunteer describes how that feels (tight throat, knot in stomach, sweaty palms). "That's natural, now what else do you know about the nuclear threat?" "I'm afraid of it, I know that . . . I'm afraid for my kids. We have 30,000 warheads right now and we're making more, three bombs a day." "What else?" . . . "and a war could be launched by computer error. There have been computer errors already, over a hundred in one year . . ." So by a form of congenial grilling, we can help each other to find out that we know a lot more than we think we do. In such an exercise a person can identify his "stupidity" and move through it to discover that there is a wealth of information inside him or her.

This exercise in a workshop can also take the form of threesomes. The three in each group take turns talking, questioning, and taking notes. A grills B: "What do you know about the nuclear threat? (or environmental destruction? or world hunger?)" As A repeats the question, B dredges up information, and C writes it down. Each takes 3 or 4 minutes in turn, and they discover how much they know — which is usually a good deal.

It is well to remember, and point out, that prowess in recalling facts and figures is not the central issue. Information can be easily manipulated. Numbers alone, as the very word suggests, are numb-ers. Our capacity to reach others stems less from our command of statistics than from our existential confrontation with the dangers of our time, from our moral outrage, from our conviction that neither we nor those who come after us should have to live under continual threats of mass annihilation. In all such conversation, we need to believe, as Gandhi did, that there is that in the other person that can hear us at the level of these deep concerns. To the extent that we can address the human being — somewhere there inside — we become effective communicators.

D/E Exercise 38
Communicating Views and Intentions
(40-60 Minutes)

It is often with the people we live and work with that we feel most blocked in communicating our concerns for the world; and that, of course, exacerbates our feelings of powerlessness. So a key aspect of empowerment work is to help us talk to the others in our lives — in a simple straightforward fashion about what we see happening to our world and what we want to do about it. Practice dialogues teach us a good deal as they surface emotions, insights, skills — and some hilarity, too. Note: this exercise is analogous to Dr. Carol Wolman's in Chapter Three, but it does not require that the guide be a trained psychotherapist.

The exercise begins by inviting ourselves to think of those people whom we consider the hardest to talk to about our pain for the world, or about the social actions we undertake. It could be our father or sister, an employer or lover, or a remote figure like the President or the Secretary of State.

We then invite role plays. "The hardest person for me to talk to is my mother," says the person who volunteers, and then chooses someone from the group who reminds him in some way of his mother. Giving this person clues and cues as to how to play the role of the mother, the volunteer begins. Perhaps it is an old conversation about why he is leafletting at the nuclear power plant. Perhaps with another participant it is an aborted defense of her views on disarmament, or an attempted explanation of why she is conducting despair and empowerment workshops instead of teaching courses in the university. And the old blocks and frustrations are re-experienced as they talk. But here in the group, at a certain point, the roles are reversed.

This reversal of roles is always revealing and productive. It breaks through our old assumptions about the person we are addressing. We may experience their confusion and fear; we may see our own self in a new light. We discover how we tend to lock people into adversary positions by our presuppositions and projections and our previous history with them. Reversing back again we continue the conversation, but are more aware now of the inner person we are addressing.

D/E Exercise 39
Neighborhood Outreach

Lee Stern, a quiet bold Quaker with the Fellowship of Reconciliation, leads workshops to help people communicate about the nuclear issue. He calls these workshops "Friendly Outreach," and about halfway through he has the participants put theory into practice by going out into the neighborhood. They ring doorbells and talk to people, asking them their concerns about nuclear weapons and nuclear war. The experience shatters many of our preconceptions about how difficult it is to talk with people beyond our immediate groups.

IV
Guiding Empowerment Rituals

Rituals that deepen our sense of power and purpose as individuals and as groups often live on in our minds longer than other interactions. In a workshop such a ritual serves to acknowledge and honor our collective journey through the challenges of the nuclear age, the discoveries and commitments we have made together, and our interconnectedness with all life. It can take many forms, using movement, silence, sound, symbols and images. Here are some forms that we have found appropriate and powerful in the work; they are arranged in a sequence, but can be used separately or in combination with other elements.

D/E Exercise 40
The Milling II
(10-40 Minutes)

This is a variation on the initial Milling exercise, described in Chapter Five. To use it now picks up that earlier motif, but with important and telling changes.

Mill about the room, without speaking, moving past each other the way you did before. Now as you pause before a person, look into each other's eyes and place your raised hands together. Let the possibility arise in your mind that the person before you may be instrumental in saving us from nuclear war . . . . Move on and mill some more. Now, as you stop again and look into the eyes of another, let yourself be aware that this person may play a central role in the healing of our world . . . .

When time permits, this milling can then take the form of brief, spoken exchanges, where at each interaction the partners affirm each other's gifts and strengths. This is particularly appropriate if the group did the exercise on *How Others Empower Us* (D/E Exercise 28) or the *Great Ball of Merit* meditation (Chapter Eight). This ritual act lets us put those insights directly into practice and to see how we can empower each other "like neurons in a neural net."

As you pause and look into another's eyes, put your hands briefly over his/her heart and then over your own. As you do, say "The powers I see in you are . . . . (name them) . . . . and I take them into myself." The other will respond with the same hand gestures, similarly reflecting, in just a sentence, the gifts he/she sees in you and can receive from you.

I don't think I have known a ritual that is more affirming to its participants.

D/E Exercise 47
Learning to See Each Other
(15 Minutes)

This guided meditation where participants face each other in pairs, makes a compelling component in an empowerment or closing ritual. It is described in Chapter Eight.

D/E Exercise 41
Affirmation of Commitment
(15 Minutes)

At the close of the above meditation or right after the empowerment milling, participants can be guided to reflect on the particular role they can play in healing our world. As they do, they bring to mind the goals that arose for them in the preceding work and their personal commitment to follow them.

Each of us has a role to play in the healing of our world. Each of us has distinctive gifts to bring. Breathing deep, closing your eyes, behold the particular conditions of your life and the particular strengths that have been given to you . . . . As you do, you know that they have been given to enable you to do something no one else can do . . . . You may not be exactly clear yet as to what that is; but the knowledge of it is within you and you can begin to open to that knowledge more and more. Listening, letting it speak to us from within, we experience our intention that it be so.

This is a moment when we allow ourselves to glimpse and affirm the uniqueness of what we can do, because of our life setting and strengths, and even because of our weaknessess and limitations. It is good to offer some ritual act to give outer form to that inner movement of intention and commitment. It could be as simple as a hand gesture, a movement forward, a lighting of a candle. Sometimes I just invite participants to put their hands over their hearts (as they listen for their inner knowing of what they are to do) and then to lower their hands in front of them, palms up, (when they feel ready to commit themselves to following it).

D/E Exercise 42

Overcoming Obstacles

(30-60 Minutes)

What obstacles are we likely to erect to keep us from following through with our commitment to heal the world? The participants are invited to consider this question, and to let their notions of what these obstacles might be come to the surface of their minds. At that point, in silence, each takes from the middle of the room a small piece of paper and a crayon, and finding a quiet spot, draws with their non-dominant hand some symbol of their particular obstacle(s). They secure it on their person as the group regathers in a large closing circle.

In the course of the words, sounds, silence that moves through the closing circle, there comes a period when the obstacles that have been identified and drawn by each participant are offered and burned. They are brought one by one to the center of the circle where a lighted candle is set in a large pan (the pan is necessary to catch the ashes and burning bits of paper). People come forward at random and in the solemnity of the act they tend to speak somewhat formally: "I, Suzanne Smith, relinquish my timidity about speaking out." "I, George Jones, hereby let go of the fear of my own feelings." One man at a recent workshop said, "My obstacle is my attachment to money," and instead of his bit of paper, he held a dollar bill into the flame.

The circle of participants generally responds as if each "burnt offering" were a gift. It often chants after each in acknowledgement and support. Sometimes the group intones "You need that no longer," sometimes it borrows from the Buddhist chant *Gaté Gaté Parasam Gaté"* or "Gone Gone Completely Gone." Occasionally someone may say "I'm not ready yet to let go of my obstacle," and there is respect in the circle for that honesty.

D/E Exercise 43

Closing Circle

(20 Minutes)

The empowerment ritual usually occurs at the end of a workshop. As described in Chapter Four, this final gathering is one where we acknowledge our interconnectedness with all our fellow-beings; it is for their sake as well as our own that we have met and worked. We take time to evoke them, spontaneously and at random, inviting them into the circle. Family members. Friends. Our babysitter. Ancestors. Unborn grandchildren. Animals. Leaders and soldiers. Russians. Nicaraguans. Prisoners and torturers. Jesus. The Buddha. The rich, the hungry, the lost. It is an opportunity to practice together our extended awareness of the vast reaches of the web of life, for it can steady us in the times that lie ahead.

The closing circle is also our opportunity to acknowledge ourselves and each other for what we permitted to happen in the workshop. "This circle will ever be part of our lives, for nothing is ever lost. The connections we've woven cannot be erased. But this is the last time we will all be physically together. Perhaps there is something that you would like to say." It is good for people to have a chance to speak at this moment, and address the whole group before it disperses; but often words are felt to be inadequate and this "saying" is done in silence, as we quietly engage each other's eyes. And it is done in sound as group members begin to sing.

Chapter Eight

Spiritual Exercises
for a Time of Apocalypse

I would not like to have the bodhisattva think this kind of work hard to achieve. If he did, there are beings beyond calculation, and he will not be able to benefit them. Let him, on the contrary, consider the work easy and pleasant, thinking they were all his mother and father and children, for this is the way to benefit all beings whose number is beyond calculation.

— **The Perfection of Wisdom in Eight Thousand Verses**

The word *apocalypse* is associated with catastrophe. We hear it increasingly used to suggest that in "facing apocalypse" we are facing disaster and the possible, even probable, end of our world. Yet the literal meaning of the word is not calamity, but revelation: the original Greek denotes *disclosure, an uncovering*. And that indeed is true of *our* situation; for the very condition of our world, with its unprecedented suffering and the portents of holocaust, can "uncover" something of enormous importance about the nature and meaning of our lives, and our relation to each other.

As we have seen in despair and empowerment work, the very act of acknowledging and moving through our *pain* for the world can reveal our *power* for the world. Countless ordinary people have experienced it in this work: that the dangers of our time can be perceived and faced in ways that release us from the isolation cell of the separate self. These perils can "truth" us to our interexistence in the web of life, and thereby open us to new dimensions of caring, courage and resilience. It does not really matter how we define these dimensions that open to us, whether we see them from a religious perspective, as grace or Christ-consciousness or Buddha-nature, or whether we understand them from a scientific perspective, as inherent in the interconnectedness of open systems. Whatever terms we use to describe them, they let us "come home" to ourselves and each other, and find in that mutual belonging a deep joy.

In a workshop, as shown with the methods in this book, we can break through to these dimensions, these vaster reaches of our being; but how do we sustain these insights in our daily lives? It is one thing to experience them in a group which is undertaking this work, and to feel there the courage, commitment and buoyancy they bring. It is another to experience them out in "the world." Our culture has conditioned us to view ourselves as separate and competitive beings; developments and encounters can "push our buttons" of fear and defensiveness. How can we experience our deep, empowering interconnectedness in situations of hardship and conflict, or even in our most immediate daily lives?

We need a "practice" — ways of reminding and refueling ourselves in the very midst of life. We need ways of tuning to our true nature and mission as we read the morning paper, go to work, choose products in the market, attend meetings, meet friends and strangers, allot our time. We need ways of being "mindful" — which as Thich Nhat Hanh says, is to be constantly aware of the miracle of being alive. Monks and saints had spiritual practices which often drew them away from the world, into seclusion. The kinds of meditative practice *we* need take us *into* the world, to let each event and encounter be the occasion for knowing the power of our interconnectedness. And each of us has a part to play in shaping these practices.

You can draw from the guided meditations in the preceding chapters, such as the *Cradling* in Chapter Five, *The Web* in Chapter Six, and the *Fantasy on Choosing Your Life* in Chapter Seven. Certain meditations, offered in workshops, have been reserved for this chapter, because participants in these workshops have found them to be the most useful in their daily lives. While they happen to derive from the Buddhist tradition, they belong to us all, as part of our planetary heritage. No belief system is necessary, only a readiness to attend to the immediacy of our own experiencing. Take them as a springboard for your own deep knowings. They will be most useful if read slowly with a quiet mind (a couple of deep breaths help) and if put directly into practice in the presence of others. You may also want to read them aloud in your family or, if alone, to speak the italicized portions into a tape recorder and then listen again with a relaxed receptive mind. They convey nothing but what we know already in the depths of our being.

D/E Exercise 44
Death Meditation

Most spiritual paths begin with the recognition of the transiency of human life. Medieval Christians honored this in the mystery play of *Everyman*. Don Juan, the Yaqui sorcerer, taught that the enlightened warrior walks with death at his shoulder. To confront and accept the inevitability of our dying releases us from attachments, frees us to live boldly, with alertness and appreciation.

An initial meditation on the Buddhist path involves reflection on the twofold fact that: "Death is certain" and "the time of death is uncertain." In our world today the thermonuclear bomb, serving in a sense as a spiritual teacher, does that meditation for us; for we all know now that we can die together at any moment, without warning. When we deliberately let the reality of that possibility surface in our consciousness, it can be painful, of course, but it also helps us rediscover some fundamental truths about life. It jolts us awake to life's vividness, its miraculous quality as something given, unearned, heightening our awareness of its beauty and the uniqueness of each object, each being.

As an occasional practice in daily life:

Look at the person you encounter (stranger, friend). *Let the realization arise in you that this person may die in a nuclear war. Keep breathing. Observe that face, unique, vulnerable . . . those eyes still can see, they are not empty sockets . . . the skin is still intact . . . . Become aware of your desire, as it arises, that this person be spared such suffering and horror, feel the strength of that desire . . . . Keep breathing . . . . Let the possibility arise in your consciousness that this may be the person you happen to be with when you die . . . that face the last you see . . . that hand the last you touch . . . . It might reach out to help you then, to comfort, to give water . . . . Open to the feelings for this person that surface in you with the awareness of this possibility. Open to the levels of caring and connection it reveals in you.*

D/E Exercise 45
Breathing Through

This simple process helps us deal with painful information, without erecting defenses and blocking it out. It is adapted from an ancient meditation for the development of compassion. Here is how it is guided in a workshop:

Relax. Center on your breathing . . . . Visualize your breath as a stream flowing up through your nose, down through windpipe, lungs. Take it down through your lungs and, picturing an opening in the bottom of your heart, visualize the breath-stream passing through your heart and out through that hole to reconnect with the larger web of life around you. Let the breath-stream, as it passes through you, appear as one loop within that vast web, connecting you with it . . . keep breathing . . .

Now open your awareness to the suffering that is present in the world.

*Drop for now all defenses and open to your knowledge of that suffering . . . .
Let it come as concretely as you can . . . concrete images of your fellow-
beings in pain and need, in fear and isolation, in prisons, hospitals,
tenements, hunger camps . . . . No need to strain for these images, they are
present to you by virtue of our interexistence. Relax and just let them surface, breathe them in . . . the vast and countless hardships of our fellow-
humans, and of our animal brothers and sisters as well, as they swim the
seas and fly the air of this ailing planet . . . . Breathe in that pain like a dark
stream, up through your nose, down through your trachea, lungs and
heart, and out again into the world net . . . . You are asked to do nothing for
now, but let it pass through your heart . . . . Keep breathing . . . . Be sure
that stream flows through and out again, don't hang on to the pain.
Surrender it for now to the healing resources of life's vast web . . . .*

*With the saint Shantideva we can say, "Let all sorrows ripen in me."
We help them ripen by passing them through our hearts . . . making good
rich compost out of all that grief . . . so we can learn from it, enhancing our
larger, collective knowing . . . .*

*If you experience an ache in the chest, a pressure within the rib cage,
that is all right. The heart that breaks open can contain the whole universe.
Your heart is that large: trust it. Keep breathing.*

This guided meditation serves to introduce the process of breathing-through,
which, once experienced, becomes useful in daily life in the many situations that
confront us with painful information. By "breathing through" the bad news, rather
than bracing ourselves against it, we can let it strengthen our sense of belonging in
the larger web of being. It helps us remain alert and open, whether reading the
newspaper, receiving criticism, or simply being present to a person who suffers.

For activists working for peace and justice, and those dealing most directly with
the griefs of our time, the practice provides protection from burn-out. Reminding us
of the collective nature of both our problems and our power, it offers a healing
measure of humility. It can also save us from self-righteousness. For when we can
take in our world's pain, accepting it as the price of our caring, we can let it inform
our acts without needing to inflict it as a punishment on others who are, at the moment, less involved. In the words of a song composed at one of my workshops,
"when the sadness seems too much / just breathe on through / we are in touch."

D/E Exercise 46
The Great Ball of Merit

Compassion, which is grief in the grief of others, is but one side of the coin. The
other side is joy in the joy of others — which in Buddhism is called *muditha.* To the

extent that we allow ourselves to identify with the sufferings of other beings, we can identify as well with their strengths. This is very important for our own sense of adequacy and resilience, because we face a time of great challenge that demands of us more commitment, endurance and courage than we can ever dredge up out of our individual supply. We can learn to draw on the other neurons in the net, and to view them, in a grateful and celebrative fashion, as so much "money in the bank."

The practice takes two forms. The one closer to the ancient Buddhist meditation is this:

> *Relax and close your eyes, relax into your breathing . . . . Open your awareness to the fellow-beings who share with you this planet-time . . . in this room . . . this neighborhood . . . this town . . . . Open to all those in this country . . . and in other lands . . . . Let your awareness encompass all beings living now in your world. Opening now to all time as well, let your awareness encompass all beings who ever lived . . . of all races and creeds and walks of life, rich, poor, kings and beggars, saints and sinners . . . . Like successive mountain ranges, the vast vistas of these fellow-beings present themselves to your mind's eye . . . .*

> *Now open yourself to the knowledge that in each of these innumerable lives some act of merit was performed. No matter how stunted or deprived the life, there was a gesture of generosity, a gift of love, an act of valor or self-sacrifice . . . on the battlefield or workplace, hospital or home . . . . From each of these beings in their endless multitudes arose actions of courage, kindness, of teaching and healing . . . . Let yourself see these manifold and immeasurable acts of merit . . . . As they arise in the vistas of your inner eye, sweep them together . . . sweep them into a pile in front of you . . . use your hands . . . pile them up . . . pile them into a heap . . . pat them into a ball. It is the Great Ball of Merit . . . . Hold it and weigh it in your hands . . . . Rejoice in it, knowing that no act of goodness is ever lost. It remains ever and always a present resource . . . a resource for the transformation of life . . . . And now, with jubilation and gratitude, you turn that great ball . . . turn it over . . . over . . . into the healing of our world.*

As we can learn from modern science and picture in the holographic model of reality, our lives interpenetrate. In the fluid tapestry of space-time there is at root no distinction between self and other. The acts and intentions of others are like seeds that can germinate and bear fruit through our own lives, as we take them into awareness and dedicate, or "turn over," that awareness to our empowerment. Thoreau, Gandhi, Martin Luther King, Dorothy Day, and the nameless heroes and heroines of our own day, all can be part of our Ball of Merit, on which we can draw for inspiration and endurance.

The second, more workaday version of the Ball of Merit meditation helps us open to the powers of others and experience synergy with them. This exercise consists of the expectant attention we bring to our encounters with other beings, viewing them with fresh openness and curiosity as to how they can enhance our Ball of Merit. We can play that inner game, whether looking at someone on the bus or across the bargaining table. It is especially useful when dealing with someone with whom we may be in conflict.

What does this person add to my Great Ball of Merit? What gifts of intellect can enrich our common store? What reserves of stubborn endurance can she or he offer? What flights of fancy or powers of love lurk behind those eyes? What kindness or courage hides in those lips, what healing in those hands?

Then, as with the breathing-through exercise, we open ourselves to the presence of these strengths, inhaling our awareness of them . . . . As our awareness grows, we experience our gratitude for them and our capacity to enhance and partake . . . .

Often we let our perceptions of the powers of others make us feel inadequate. Beside the eloquent colleague, we can feel inarticulate; in the presence of an athlete we can feel weak and clumsy; in the process, we can come to resent both our self and the other person with whom we compare ourselves.

In the light of the Great Ball of Merit, however, the gifts and good fortunes of others appear, not as judgments, put-downs or competing challenges, but as resources we can honor and take pleasure in. We can learn to play detective, spying out, from even the unlikeliest material, treasures for the enhancement of life. Like air and sun and water, they form part of our common good.

In addition to releasing us from the mental cramp of envy, this spiritual practice — or game — offers two other rewards. One is pleasure in our own acuity, as our merit-detecting ability improves. And the second is the response of others, who, though ignorant of the game we are playing, sense something in our manner that invites them to move more openly into the person they can be.

D/E Exercise 47
Learning to See Each Other

This exercise is derived from the Buddhist practice known as the Brahmaviharas, or the Four Abodes of the Buddha, which are lovingkindness, compassion, joy in the joy of others, and equanimity. Adapted for use in a social context, it helps us to see each other more truly and experience the depths of our interconnections.

In workshops I offer this as a guided meditation, with participants sitting in pairs facing each other. At its close I encourage them to proceed to use it, or any portion they like, as they go about the business of their daily lives. It is an excellent antidote to boredom, when our mind is idling and our eye falls on another person, say on the subway or waiting in line at the check-out counter. It charges that idle movement with beauty and discovery. It also is useful when dealing with people we are tempted to dislike or disregard, for it breaks open our accustomed ways of viewing them. When used like this, as a meditation-in-action, one does not, of course, gaze long and deeply into the other's eyes, as in the guided exercise. A seemingly casual glance is enough, or the simple exchange of buying stamps or toothpaste — any occasion, in other words, that permits us to be present to another human being.

The guided, group form goes like this:

Sit in pairs. Face each other. Stay silent. Take a couple of deep breaths, centering yourself and exhaling tension. Look into each other's eyes. If you feel discomfort or an urge to laugh or look away, just note that embarrassment with patience and gentleness toward yourself and come back, when you can, to your partner's eyes. You may never see this person again: the opportunity to behold the uniqueness of this particular human being is given to you now.

As you look into this being's eyes, let yourself become aware of the powers that are there . . . . Open yourself to awareness of the gifts and strengths and the potentialities in this being . . . . Behind those eyes are unmeasured reserves of ingenuity and endurance, of wit and wisdom. There are gifts there, of which this person him/her-self is unaware. Consider what these untapped powers can do for the healing of our planet and the relishing of our common life . . . . As you consider that, let yourself become aware of your desire that this person be free from fear . . . . Let yourself experience how much you want this being to be free from hatred . . . and free from greed . . . and free from sorrow . . . and the causes of suffering . . . . Know that what you are now experiencing is the great lovingkindness . . . . It is good for building a world.

Now, as you look into those eyes, let yourself become aware of the pain that is there. There are sorrows accumulated in that life's journey . . . . There are failures and losses, griefs and disappointments beyond the telling . . . . Let yourself open to them, open to that pain . . . to hurts that this person may never have shared with another being . . . . What you are now experiencing is the great compassion. It is good for the healing of our world.

As you look into those eyes, open to the thought of how good it would be to make common cause . . . . Consider how ready you might be to work together . . . to take risks in a joint venture . . . . Imagine the zest of that, the excitement and laughter of engaging on a common project . . . acting boldly and trusting each other . . . . As you open to that possibility, what you open to is the great wealth: the pleasure in each other's powers, the joy in each other's joy.

Lastly now, let your awareness drop deep, deep within you like a stone, sinking below the level of what words or acts can express . . . . Breathe deep and quiet . . . . Open your consciousness to the deep web of relationship that underlies and interweaves all experiencing, all knowing . . . . It is the web of life in which you have taken being and in which you are supported . . . out of that vast web you cannot fall . . . no stupidity or failure, no personal inadequacy, can ever sever you from that living web, for that is what you are . . . and what has brought you into being . . . feel the assurance of that knowledge. Feel the great peace . . . rest in it . . . . Out of that great peace, we can venture everything. We can trust. We can act.

This meditation in the form it is given here first happened at a conference in Holland on world development. Among the 35 who were present at an evening workshop were two men: one was a German professor and the other a Dutch farmer who had fought the Nazis in World War II. Earlier in the conference they had expressed contrary opinions about a report from the Chinese delegation, and finding themselves in conflict, they were no longer on speaking terms. To their mutual consternation they found themselves paired off together as partners in this guided meditation. The next morning I walked into the plenary session to find them sitting side by side, one's arm around the other's shoulders as they studied the day's agenda. Seeing me, the Dutch farmer jumped up and came over "I must tell you," he said, "what happened last night." At first, he said, when he and the German were asked to look into each other's eyes, there was in each a wall of defiance, like two boys in a staring contest. Like an iron curtain, it stayed there during the section on lovingkindness when they were asked to see each other's gifts. But when they were invited to open to each other's pain, to the old hurts they had suffered since childhood, "that wall crumbled," he said. "Our eyes, or something behind our eyes, came together, like this (he interlocked his fingers). It was good we did not have to speak, for what can words say? And then we knew that we could work together. There is much that we must do."

In doing this exercise we realize that we do not have to be particularly noble or saintlike in order to wake up to the power of our oneness with other beings. In our time, that simple awakening is the gift the bomb holds for us. For all its horror and stupidity the Bomb is also the manifestation of an awesome spiritual truth — the truth about the hell we create for ourselves when we cease to learn how to love. Saints, mystics, and prophets throughout the ages saw that law; now *all* can see it and none can escape its consequences.

For us to regard the Bomb (or the dying seas, the poisoned air) as a monstrous injustice to us would suggest that we never took seriously the injunction to love. Perhaps we thought all along that spiritual teachings were meant only for saints. But now we see, as an awful revelation, that we are *all* called to be saints — not good necessarily, or pious or devout, but saints in the sense of just loving each other.

It is in that possibility that we can take heart. Even in confusion and fear, with all our fatigues and petty faults, we can let that awareness work in and through our lives. Such simple exercises, as those offered here, can help us to do that, and to begin to see ourselves and each other with fresh eyes.

Let me close with the same suggestion that closes our workshops. It is a practice that is corollary to the earlier death meditation, where we recognize that the person we meet may die in a nuclear war. Look at the person you see. It may be someone else (lover, child, co-worker, postman . . .), or your own face in the mirror. Regard him or her with the recognition that:

> *This person before me may be instrumental in saving us from nuclear war. In this person are gifts for the healing of our planet. In him/her are powers that can redound to the joy of all beings.*

Postscript

In the play *The Last Yiddish Poet*, the protagonist, traveling through history, finds himself in the Third Reich. Looking out over the grey landscape he sees the smoking chimneys of Auschwitz, Dachau . . . and is told what is happening there. In horror and grief he cries to his companion, "I don't know whether to prepare to live or prepare to die!" And his companion, a rabbi, says, "I think it is the same thing."

That is what we discover in despair and empowerment work. The very perils that present us with imminent possibilities of mass annihilation can teach us how to live. If we face them consciously and openly together, we rediscover in our shared humanity the wellsprings of our caring and our courage. And that caring and courage begin to reach into every part of our lives — into the ways we see each other and the ways we use our time and energy.

We hear it said that we live in an end-time — not because the death of our species is certain, but because, for the first time in history, it is now possible. As we let that fact sink in, we find there is one great virtue to living in an end-time: it allows our deepest authenticities to emerge. As many learn, facing their own personal death, that encounter can empower us to discover and express at last who we really are. It rips away the veil of familiarity that has cloaked our days, a veil woven by social distances and soporific routines, by the conventions and compromises of business-as-usual.

In the last act of *Our Town* Emily Webb, who died in childbirth, asks for the privilege of reliving just one day of her life. She chooses her twelfth birthday and walks back into her home, sees it just as it was — the stove, the kitchen table, her mother cooking and calling the family to breakfast. She sees her twelve-year-old self come down the stairs, preoccupied with her clothing, hurrying to get to school. The Emily from the grave beholds the precious, poignant beauty of each face, each gesture — and shouts to her family to stop, stop and see, stop and look. Look at each other! Behold the gift. But they cannot hear her.

The Bomb's gift for us now is to help us see each other — each one of us, each unrepeatable gesture, each vanishing moment. Mortal as we are, we cannot, finally, ask more than that: to be present moment by moment to the miracle of being alive. In that act of presence, we find our authenticity, our wholeness. And in that wholeness — which is the meaning of holiness, too — is our capacity to take risk, and a kind of joy.

The gift, I think, is a greater one, yet. It extends beyond our individual capacity for appreciation or even courage. For the connections we now weave, as we awaken together to save our planet, allow a new social, even planetary level of awareness to arise. As we saw in Chapter Two, we participate, like neurons in a neural net, in the emergence of a collective dimension of consciousness. That emergence seems essential now to our survival. And even though we can glimpse it only dimly — as through a glass darkly — each act, each encounter can further that evolutionary development.

Despair and empowerment work, therefore, is consciousness-raising in the truest sense of the term. It increases our awareness not only of the perils that face us, but also of the promise inherent in the human heart. Whether we "make it" or not, whether our efforts to heal our world succeed or fail, we live then in so vivid a consciousness of our community that the most obvious and accurate word for it is love. And that seems, in and of itself, a fulfillment.

Appendix A
Sample Agendas

Each workshop is unique, reflecting the distinctive mix of participants, the style of the facilitator, the choice of methods used. These include methods described in this book and others that are similar. Each workshop, however, to be effective, moves in the direction suggested by the plotline described in Chapter Four. To illustrate this movement, and how exercises can be sequenced to support it, here are some sample agendas.

Short Half-day or Evening Workshop

Agenda	Approximate Duration in Minutes	D/E Exercise Number
Variation 1 *(Approx. 3 Hours)*		
Opening Out / Tuning In	5	7
Opening Remarks	15	
Introductory Sharings	15	8
Milling	10	9
Open Sentences	30	10
Cradling	30	13
Break	15	
Large Group Discussion on Power	20	17
Guided Meditation	10	47
Closing Circle	5-10	43
Variation 2 *(Approx. 2½ Hours)*		
Relaxation	5	
Opening Remarks	15	
Introductions	5	
Nuclear Stories	40	11
Break	15	
Large Group Discussion on Power	20	17
A Future Visioning Exercise	30	37, 35
Guided Meditation	10	29, 25
Closing Circle	5-10	43

Daylong Workshop

Agenda	Approximate Duration in Minutes	D/E Exercise Number
Music and Opening Out	10	7
Opening Remarks	15	
Participant Introductions	15	
Film, Flip charts, Slide Show, or Talk on D/E	30	
Personal Sharing	15	
Small Groups	15	
Milling	10	9
Open Sentences	30	10
Cradling	30	13
(Break for Lunch)	60	
Brainstorm	10	18
Mini-Lecture	20	17
Experiencing Our Power	30	26, 27
Small Group Discussions	60	
Communication Exercise	30-40	37, 38
Evaluation and Follow-up	30	
Guided Meditation	10	46, 47, 32
Closing Circle	10	43

Weekend Workshop

Agenda	Approximate Duration in Minutes	D/E Exercise Number
Friday Night		
Music	10	
Opening Out / Tuning In	10	7, 21, 22
Opening Remarks	20	
General Introductions	20	
Nuclear Stories	60	11
Saturday		
Small Group Check-in	15	
Talk on D/E	20	
Milling	10	9
Open Sentences	30	10
Imaging with Colors or Cradling	60	13, 14
(Lunch Break)		
Small Group Check-in	20	
"I Don't Care" Exercise	15	15
Despair Ritual	90	16
(Dinner Break)		
Small Group Check-in	30	
Spontaneous Writing	30	19
Communication Role Plays	30	37, 38
Music and Dancing	. . .	
Sunday		
Small Group Check-in	15	
The Well	60	20
Mini-lecture on Power	15	17
Imaging a World Without Weapons	90	33
(Lunch Break)		
Gen. Discussion on Plans for Follow-up	40	
Evaluation of Workshop	10	
Empowerment Ritual	45	40, 41, 42, 43

Appendix B
Sample Announcements

A despair and empowerment workshop combines cognitive, emotional and spiritual work as it addresses our global concerns. Because it does not fit easily into pre-existing categories of group work, it can be hard to convey in a brief announcement. Here are a few descriptions of past workshops.

TITLE: Waking Up in the Nuclear Age

Everyone, no matter what his or her political stance, lives with the threat of nuclear holocaust. This workshop helps us prepare inwardly and outwardly for living in a precarious world and facing future crises. It is designed to bring us together for common survival . . . to help us move beyond psychic numbing, explore our feelings and ideas about the nuclear threat, and find more loving and creative ways to work for change.

(Chellis Glendinning)

TITLE: Despair and Empowerment in the Nuclear Age

In this workshop participants will share their concerns about the planetary crisis. Through experiential work, lecture and discussion sessions, they will: explore the physical, emotional and spiritual costs to individuals, families and communities of living with nuclear weapons; learn theory and methodology for assisting ourselves and others in dealing with the anguish and isolation of living on a threatened planet; experience peacemaking as processes of healing and empowerment.

(Joanna Macy and Sarah Pirtle)

TITLE: For Teachers, Healers and Other Care-givers

In this day-long session we will look at the threat of nuclear annihilation as the most insidious cultural and psychological disturbance of the twentieth century . . . . As all healers know, it is the presence of pain — whether physical or emotional — which mobilizes people to engage in the healing process. And, as all good teachers know, people who are disturbed have difficulty assimilating information and thinking well . . . . This is an opportunity for healers, teachers and other care-givers to experience and release painful emotions tied to living in the nuclear age, to discuss the theory of this process, and reflect on how it can be used in situations with clients, patients, students and others.

(Kit Bricca, Barbara Hazard, Joy Marcus, Kevin McVeigh)

TITLE: Taking Heart in the Nuclear Age

Being conscious in our world today involves awareness of unprecedented human suffering and growing possibilities of global disaster. How can we live with this awareness without feeling overwhelmed? How can we find resilience and courage? As the dangers to planetary survival escalate, we need ways to deal with our innermost responses to world crisis so we can overcome psychic numbing, exhaustion and despair. In this workshop we will share what is in our hearts about the state of our planet. Through this personal sharing, guided meditation, bodywork and ritual, we will explore and move through our pain for the world to find deeper levels of community, commitment, and even joy. The workshop will offer methods to release energy for creative action, and to organize ongoing supsupport groups for personal and social change.

(Joanna Macy)

TITLE: Women in the Nuclear Age

This is what we think is so: there is in each of us a great warrior — not a person of violence or a military soldier, but one who is gentle and tough, a powerful woman who loves deeply and fights for what she believes in. At this moment our most critical task is to prevent nuclear war and ensure the continuity of life on the planet. This workshop will focus on the warrior within: the one who speaks and is heard, who believes in herself and knows her power to make political change. In this workshop we will do emotional work as well as practical problem solving. (Barbara Hazard and Joy Marcus)

TITLE: Living in the Nuclear Age

This workshop consists of exercises which enable us to experience our feelings about nuclear war and to discover and tell our own "nuclear stories" — the stories of our lives as affected by the nuclear threat. It includes a discussion of what to do about the situation and how not to go crazy in a nuclear world.   (Charles Varon and Frances Peavey)

TITLE: Transforming the Nuclear Dragon: from Despair to Empowerment

The bridge from inner fear and despair to empowerment and action is built by many hands. By participating in this workshop you are, in a sense, joining millions throughout this planet who are vitally involved in stopping the threat of a nuclear holocaust. We will use small group and dyadic interactions; guided fantasy and individual work; all in the service of facing our fear and psychic numbing around the issue of the nuclear threat. By helping each other to transform the dragon of despair and paralysis within, we empower ourselves to move against the nuclear dragon residing without.   (Howard Hamburger and Frank Rubenfeld)

Appendix C
Resources
(A partial listing)

I

Organizations and Programs

1. For further guidance and materials in conducting despair and empowerment work, for information on training programs, and for leaders and speakers, address the following organizations:

    •   Interhelp (330 Ellis St., Rm. 505, San Francisco, CA 94102, 415-673-5433). Inquire through the national office for regional and local contacts. This is a nonpartisan network interlinking groups and individuals involved in despair and empowerment work, including the organizations listed below. It also offers:

        — *Humpty Dumpty Report*, a bimonthly newsletter detailing resources and work in progress (where some of the methods offered in this book first appeared).

        — *Evolutionary Blues*, a journal looking at the change of consciousness required by the threat of nuclear war.

        — The Fran and Charlie Nuclear Comedy Team, which performs in the U.S. and abroad and engages people in despair and empowerment work through laughter.

    •   Waking Up in the Nuclear Age (Box 23, Fort Mason Center, San Francisco, CA 94123, 415-928-2014). This organization, dedicated to consciousness-raising, psychological support and personal and political empowerment, offers despair and empowerment workshops, trainings for mental health professionals in dealing with the nuclear threat, consultations, conferences and speakers.

    •   Psychotherapists for Social Responsibility (152 Anza St., Fremont CA 94539, 415-490-5788), an organization of mental health workers dedicated to the eradication of the threat of nuclear war.

    •   The Despairwork Movement in Great Britian (West Lynn, Dalry, Ayrshire KA24 4LJ Scotland, c/o Paul Fink and Mary Simister). This network offers workshops and a newsletter, *Threads*.

2. Other organizations and programs dealing with interpersonal, psychological and spiritual dimensions of the planetary crisis include:

- Association for Humanistic Psychology (324 9th St., San Francisco, CA 94103)
- Hardscrabble Hill Center for Women (Box 130, Orland, ME 04472)
- Imaging a World without Weapons (c/o Lee Stern, 57 Fourth Ave., Nyack, NY 10960)
- The New Manhattan Project, American Friends Service Committee, 15 Rutherford Place, New York, NY 10003)
- Parenting in the Nuclear Age (6501 Telegraph Ave., Oakland, CA 94609)
- Psychologists for Social Responsibility (1841 Columbia Rd., N.W., Suite 206, Washington D.C. 20009)
- World Peacemakers (2852 Ontario Rd., N.W., Washington D.C. 20009)

3. For an extensive listing of peace organizations, refer to *Handbook: Arms Control and Peace Organizations/Activities*, Dec. 1982, the Forum Institute, 1225 15th St., N.W., Washington D.C. 20005)

II

Written Materials

The following books, publications and articles are useful in dealing with the psychological and spiritual aspects of the present planetary crisis:

Amen, Carol, "The Last Testament," *Ms. Magazine*, August 1981.

American Psychiatric Association, *Task Force 20: Psychosocial Aspects of Nuclear Developments*, 1982 (American Psychiatric Association, 1700 18th St., N.W., Washington D.C. 20009).

Benson, Bernard, *The Peace Book*, New York: Bantam Books, 1980.

Dabrowski, Kazimierz, *Positive Disintegration*, New York: Little, Brown, 1964.

Dammann, Erik, *The Future in Our Hands*, Oxford: Pergamon Press, 1979.

Douglass, James W., *Lightning East and West*, Sunburst Press, 1980 (Box 6, 4610 S.E. Belmont, Portland, OR 97215).

Educators for Social Responsibility, *Creating Our Future*, 1982 (ESR, 639 Massachusetts Ave., Cambridge, MA 02139).

Evolutionary Blues, Interhelp (330 Ellis St., Rm. 505, San Francisco, CA 94102).

Fisher, Roger, "Preventing Nuclear War," *Bulletin of Atomic Scientists*, March 1981.

Frank, Jerome, *Sanity and Survival, Psychological Aspects of War and Peace*, New York: Vantage Press, 1967.

Glendinning, Chellis, "Telling our Nuclear Stories," *Fellowship* Magazine, Nov. 1981.

Global Education Associates, "Spirituality and World Order," Whole Earth Papers, No. 16, 1982 (GEA 552 Park Ave., East Orange, NJ 07017).

Grannis, J.C., Laffin, A.J., Schade, E., *The Risk of the Cross, Christian Discipleship in the Nuclear Age*, New York: Seabury Press, 1981.

Grassie, William, "Dealing with Dread," *Fellowship* Magazine, Jan./Feb. 1981.

Group for Advancement of Psychiatry (GAP) Report #57, "Psychiatric Aspects of the Prevention of Nuclear War," 1964 (American Psychiatric Association, 1700 18th St., N.W., Washington D.C. 20009).

Interhelp, *Humpty Dumpty Report*, newsletter (330 Ellis St., Rm. 505, San Francisco, CA 94102).

Jampolsky, G.G. ed., *Children As Teachers of Peace*, Millbrae, CA: Celestial Arts, 1982.

Keyes, Ken Jr., *The Hundredth Monkey*, Vision Books, 1981 (St. Mary, KY 40063).

Koen, Susan and Nina Swaim, *Ain't Nowhere We Can Run: A Handbook on the Nuclear Mentality*, Wand, 1980 (Box 421, Norwich, VT 05055).

Laszlo, Ervin, *The Inner Limits of Mankind*, Oxford: Pergamon Press, 1979.

_____., *The Systems View of the World*, New York: George Braziller, 1972.

Lifton, Robert J., *The Broken Connection*, New York: Simon and Schuster, 1979.

_____., *Death in Life: Survivors of Hiroshima*, New York: Random House, 1968.

_____., and Richard Falk, *Indefensible Weapons*, New York: Basic Books, 1982.

Mack, John E., "Psychological Effects of the Arms Race," *Bulletin of Atomic Scientists*, April 1981.

Macy, Joanna R., *Despairwork*, Philadelphia: New Society Publishers, 1982.

_____., *Dharma and Development*, West Hartford, CT: Kumarian Press, 1982.

McAllister, Pam, ed., *Reweaving the Web of Life: Feminism and Nonviolence*, Philadelphia: New Society Publishers, 1982).

McGinnis, Kathleen and James, *Parenting for Peace and Justice*, Maryknoll, NY: Orbis Books, 1982.

Pastoral Letter of the American Bishops, "The Challenge of Peace: God's Promise and Our Response," Origins, NC News Service (1312 Massachusetts Ave., N.W., Washington D.C. 20005).

Physicians for Social Responsibility, *Speaking Out on the Threat of Nuclear War*, 1982 (Greater Boston PSR, 639 Massachusetts Ave., Cambridge, MA 02139).

Quinn, Archbishop John R., "Making Peace in a Nuclear Age," *St. Anthony Messenger*, 1982 (Catholic Update, 1615 Republic St., Cincinnati, OH 45210).

Russell, Peter, *The Global Brain: Speculations on the Evolutionary Leap to Planetary Consciousness*, Los Angeles: J.P. Tarcher, 1982.

Schell, Jonathan, *The Fate of the Earth*, New York: Alfred A. Knopf, 1982.

Schwebel, Milton, ed. *Behavioral Science and Human Survival*, Palo Alto: Science and Behavior Books, 1965 (See articles by Sybille K. Escalona, "Children and the Threat of Nuclear War," and Milton Schwebel, "Nuclear Cold War: Student Opinion and Professional Responsibility.")

Sojourners, *A Matter of Faith*, a study guide for churches on the arms race (P.O. Box 29272, Washington D.C. 20017).

Starhawk, *Dreaming the Dark*, Boston: Beacon Press, 1982.

Traprock Peace Center, *Facing the Facts*, 1982. A series of educational flipcharts on the nuclear threat and our responses (Box 145, Greenfield, MA 01302).

III

Audio-Visual Materials

Films, tapes, slide shows and flip charts can be very useful in despair and empowerment workshops, providing a common experience relating to the condition of our world and evoking responses. Some of those we have used in, or in connection with, the workshops include:

Dark Circle, produced and directed by Judy Irving, Chris Beaver and Ruth Landy, 1982. 82 minutes. This documentary follows several people as they discover the effects of plutonium on their lives and take action. (Independent Documentary Group, 394 Elizabeth St., San Francisco, CA 94114.)

Day After Trinity: J. Robert Oppenheimer and the Atomic Bomb, directed by Jon Else, 1981. 90 minutes. Oppenheimer's role in the development of the atomic bomb and his struggle against it in the years after its use. (Pyramid Films, Box 1048, Santa Monica, CA 90406.)

Eight Minutes to Midnight, produced by Mary Benjamin, 1981. Portrait of Dr. Helen Caldicott in action on the nuclear issue. (Direct Cinema Ltd., Box 315, Franklin Lakes, NJ 07417.)

Facing the Facts, Traprock Peace Center, 1982. A series of educational flipcharts on the nuclear threat and our responses. (Box 145, Greenfield, MA 01302.)

Growing Up in the Nuclear Shadow, produced by Ian and Eric Thiermann and Vivienne Verdon-Roe, 1983. 25 minutes. 27 children and young people express their thoughts and feelings about the nuclear threat. (Educational Film and Video Project, 1725 B Seabright Ave., Santa Cruz, CA 95062.)

I Have a Nuclear War Inside Me, produced by Educators for Social Responsibility, 1982. Elementary and highschool students meet in their classrooms with Roberta Snow and Eric Chivian of ESR to share their thoughts and fears about nuclear weapons. (ESR, 639 Massachusetts Ave., Cambridge, MA 02139.)

The Last Epidemic, produced by Ian and Eric Thiermann in 1982. 35 minutes. The jolting documentary summary of the Physicians for Social Responsibility symposium in San Francisco in 1980, entitled "Medical Effects of Nuclear War." (Available through Physicians for Social Responsibility, 639 Massachusetts Ave., Cambridge, MA 02139).

MAD: The Psychology of Nuclear Armament, slide-tape show by Norman MacLeod for International Physicians to Prevent Nuclear War, 1982. 17 minutes. A study in voices and pictures of the psychological effects of the nuclear arms race. (Peace Resource Center, Wilmington College, Pyle Center, Box 1183, Wilmington, OH 45177.)

No Frames No Boundaries, produced by Creative Initiative. 21 minutes. Visually beautiful, it inspires appreciation for our planet as an organic whole and the extent to which it is threatened by nuclear weapons. (Creative Initiative, 222 High St., Palo Alto, CA 94310.)

No Other Generation, produced by Original Face Video. 30 minutes. Spiritual leaders, speakers and participants in the historic 1981 "Meeting of the Ways" address the spiritual dimensions of the planetary crisis. (Association for Humanistic Psychology, 325 9th St., San Francisco, CA 94103.)

The War Game, directed by Peter Watkins for BBC, 1966. 50 minutes. A bleak and powerful dramatization of the immediate aftermath of a nuclear attack on Great Britain. (Contemporary McGraw Hill, 1221 Avenue of the Americas, New York, NY 10020.)

War Without Winners, directed by Haskell Wexler for the Center for Defense Information, 1979. 28 minutes. An appeal to reason about the arms race, it juxtaposes views of military experts and ordinary people in the U.S. and the U.S.S.R. (Films, Inc., 733 Green Bay Road, Wilmette, IL 60091.)

For additional audio-visual resources write for the "Media Network-Guide to Disarmament Media," which lists 26 films, videotapes and slide shows as well as several other guides to nuclear films and a list of film libraries. (Media Network, 208 W. 13th St., New York, NY 10011.)

NOTE: Before showing these films, especially outside of a workshop setting, please read "Helping People Deal with Terrifying Films" (Appendix D).

Appendix D

Helping People Deal With Terrifying Films

by Frances Peavey

(Frances wrote this piece in November 1981 as a guide for people involved in doing public work around nuclear war issues. It details human ways to show terrifying films or videotapes to audiences.)

1. Announce film "business" before film is shown: "You can buy this film or rent it. Over at the table you can find brochures and information on how to buy or rent the film, etc." Do *not* try to sell the film after the film.

2. If possible, help people get to know each other a bit before the film. "Can we go around and tell our names and something we like to do or something we enjoyed recently," or "Give your name and a little something about why you came to see this film."

    Some groups are too large: "Before we start, talk to a person in a seat near you and tell them a little about who you are and why you came tonight."

3. Introduce the film (or video) in a friendly, connected way. Try to avoid hysteria. Be honest and open-hearted. Give whatever speech you want to give before the film, not after.

4. Before the film begins, let people know how they will have a chance to talk about it when it's over. Several methods that have been effective, given limited time, are:

    a. In a large group: "After the film, there will be 10 to 20 minutes for you to talk with the people sitting around you about the film and how you feel. It's important that we don't face this threatening future alone, so take the opportunity to share even if it's with someone you don't know well. We're all in this together." Take a few minutes for people to arrange groups of four or five.

    b. "Following the film, we will divide into groups to discuss how we feel and what we should do. Let's set up those groups now so we can get into them. Please don't just go off by yourself and feel sunk. We're all going to have to work together to solve this mess. Try to use this opportunity to share what's in your heart and your ideas with us." Divide the room into groups.

    c. "Some people may have questions of an informational nature and others may want to talk about how they feel. Let's set up those groups now so that immediately following the film we can start working on the next steps. Whichever group you go to is up to you. There are going to be many different approaches to this situation and our survival is dependent upon all of the approaches in order to turn this situation around. Have people raise hands for "feeling" groups, count off in groups of four or five and assign an after-the-film meeting place.

5. Show the film. One possible way of using films in small groups that is sometimes useful is to encourage people to shut off the projector in the midst of the showing and talk about how they feel and ask questions. Then when people start to go numb or feel strong feelings, they can stop the film and talk. Also, the leader can decide to turn the projector off initially and ask people to talk. There is no reason to see a film straight through and be so numb that you cannot absorb the last half of the film. People need to practice shutting machines off when the human costs become too great.

6. Do not stand up after the film is over and try to scare people with further horrifying facts. This is a violent act and does not encourage peace. When people are subjected to too much fear-provoking material, they tend toward numbing, forgetting or feeling so violated that they are hostile to the overall message.

7. Watch for people who are unusually troubled and ask someone to help them by listening to them or just being with them.

8. When we are dealing with the current threatening world situation, we are dealing with the heaviest grief, angers and fears we all carry with us. They're powerful feelings which need to be respected in a caring way. This enables people to act from power, not to shut down and become paralyzed.

9. Some groups are more comfortable writing their thinking and feelings in privacy and then sharing their writing with a small group. This is often most effective with groups which are not so accustomed to talking with people outside their family. Writing may actually free some people to express their inner feelings.

10. Take care of yourself. Talk about what's in your heart and how you feel about the information in the films and your own fears. Don't depend on talking in the showings to work through your own fear. Develop your own support group of people who are also doing this work and struggling with the feelings it brings up. Do not do this work in isolation.

Notes

Chapter One

1. Robert J. Lifton, *The Broken Connection*, New York: Simon and Schuster, 1979; p. 338.

2. John E. Mack, "A Context for Destruction — or Connection," *The Graduate Review*, March/April 1981.

3. Christina Robb in the *Boston Globe*, January 24, 1982.

4. Peter Marin, "Living in Moral Pain," *Psychology Today*, November 1981.

5. Robert Murphy, M.D. "The Psychology of Despair and Empowerment," Physicians for Social Responsibility, Sheridan, Wyoming; unpublished mss.

6. Leon Balter, "Overview of Project on Attitudes Toward Nuclear War by the Colloquium of Psychoanalysts and Social Scientists," reprinted by the New York Yearly Meeting Peace Institute, Powell House, Old Chatham, NY, June 1979.

7. George F. Kennan, address at Dartmouth College, November 11, 1981, *Boston Globe*, November 29, 1981.

8. Balter, *Ibid.*

9. Dorothee Soelle, *Suffering*, Philadelphia: Fortress Press, 1975; p. 36

Chapter Two

1. Gregory Bateson, *Steps to an Ecology of Mind*, New York: Ballantine Books, 1972; p. 482.

2. Norbert Weiner, *The Human Use of Human Beings*, New York: Avon Books, 1967; p. 130

3. Jacob Needleman, *A Sense of the Cosmos: the Encounter of Modern Science and Ancient Truth*, New York: Dutton, 1977.

Chapter Three

1. John E. Mack, "Impact on Children and Adolescents of Nuclear Developments," American Psychiatric Association Task Force 20, Psychosocial Aspects of Nuclear Developments, 1982; p. 89.

Chapter Four

1. Erik Erikson, *Young Man Luther*, New York: W.W. Norton, 1958; p. 7.

2. Elissa Melamed, "Travailler avec l'Angoisse Planétaire," *Co-Evolution #6*, Paris, Autumn 1981. (Also in English version: *Fellowship* Magazine, April-May 1982.)

Chapter Five

1. Lewis Mumford, "The Morals of Extermination," *Atlantic Monthly*, October 1959.

2. Chellis Glendinning, "Telling our Nuclear Stories," *Fellowship Magazine*, November 1981.

3. *Ibid.*

4. Jack Belden, *China Shakes the World*, N.Y. Monthly Review Press, 1949, pp. 487-8.

If you like this book,
New Society Publishers invites you
to take a look at our other products.

DESPAIRWORK: AWAKENING TO THE PERIL AND PROMISE OF OUR TIME

by Joanna Macy

"What we urgently need is to break the taboo against expressions of despair for our world—to validate these feelings of rage and grief, realize their universality, and experience in them the mutual support that can empower us to act. To do despair-work is, in a real sense, to wake up—both to the peril and the promise."

32 pp. 1982 ISBN 0-86571-023-6 $2.45

BUILDING SOCIAL CHANGE COMMUNITIES

by the Training/Action Affinity Group

Build the social change community you need to aid you in your personal growth, social activism. How to: resolve conflicts creatively, facilitate meetings, make group decisions, form shared households, build networks for social change.

105 pages. Illustrated. ISBN 0-86571-005-8 $3.95

OFF THEIR BACKS... AND ON OUR OWN TWO FEET

by Men Against Patriarchy

This pamphlet addressed to men includes three essays: "More Power Than We Want: Masculine Sexuality and Violence," "Understanding and Fighting Sexism," and "Overcoming Masculine Oppression In Mixed Groups."

32 pages. 1983. ISBN 0-86571-028-7 $2.45

TWO ESSAYS: ON ANGER and NEW MEN, NEW WOMEN Some Thoughts on Nonviolence

by Barbara Deming

Thought-provoking essays adding new depth to the slogan that 'the personal is political.' Modern classics in the literature of nonviolent struggle, challenging us to recreate ourselves even as we attempt to recreate our world. Originally appeared in Barbara Deming's *We Can Not Live Without Our Lives.*

32 pp. 1982. ISBN: 0-86571-024-4 $2.45

HANDBOOK FOR SATYAGRAHIS: A MANUAL FOR VOLUNTEERS OF TOTAL REVOLUTION

by Narayan Desai

India's foremost trainer in nonviolent action presents an integrated, practical approach to training for radical social change, growing out of the experience of the Gandhian movement.

57 pp. ISBN: 0-86571-003-1 $3.95

DE-DEVELOPING THE U.S. THROUGH NONVIOLENCE

by William Moyer

This document predicts the shape of future anti-nuclear movement; grapples with relations between U.S. economic patterns and growing world scarcities and threats to ecosphere. More relevant with each passing year.

12 pages. 35¢

A Call to Stop the Cruise and Pershing II
10¢ plus SASE $9/100 postpaid